T0215095

Practical Software Development Techniques

Tools and Techniques for Building Enterprise Software

Edward Crookshanks

Apress®

Practical Software Development Techniques: Tools and Techniques for Building Enterprise Software

ISBN-13 (pbk): 978-1-4842-0729-1

ISBN-13 (electronic): 978-1-4842-0728-4

Trademarked names, logos, and images may appear in this book. Rather than use a trademark symbol with every occurrence of a trademarked name, logo, or image we use the names, logos, and images only in an editorial fashion and to the benefit of the trademark owner, with no intention of infringement of the trademark.

The use in this publication of trade names, trademarks, service marks, and similar terms, even if they are not identified as such, is not to be taken as an expression of opinion as to whether or not they are subject to proprietary rights.

While the advice and information in this book are believed to be true and accurate at the date of publication, neither the authors nor the editors nor the publisher can accept any legal responsibility for any errors or omissions that may be made. The publisher makes no warranty, express or implied, with respect to the material contained herein.

Managing Director: Welmoed Spahr
Lead Editor: James DeWolf
Development Editor: Douglas Pundick
Editorial Board: Steve Anglin, Mark Beckner, Ewan Buckingham, Gary Cornell,
    Louise Corrigan, Jim DeWolf, Jonathan Gennick, Jonathan Hassell, Robert Hutchinson,
    Michelle Lowman, James Markham, Matthew Moodie, Jeff Olson, Jeffrey Pepper,
    Douglas Pundick, Ben Renow-Clarke, Dominic Shakeshaft, Gwenan Spearing,
    Matt Wade, Steve Weiss
Coordinating Editor: Kevin Walter
Compositor: SPi Global
Indexer: SPi Global
Artist: SPi Global
Cover Designer: Anna Ishchenko

Distributed to the book trade worldwide by Springer Science+Business Media New York, 233 Spring Street, 6th Floor, New York, NY 10013. Phone 1-800-SPRINGER, fax (201) 348-4505, e-mail orders-ny@springer-sbm.com, or visit www.springeronline.com. Apress Media, LLC is a California LLC and the sole member (owner) is Springer Science + Business Media Finance Inc (SSBM Finance Inc). SSBM Finance Inc is a **Delaware** corporation.

For information on translations, please e-mail rights@apress.com, or visit www.apress.com.

Apress and friends of ED books may be purchased in bulk for academic, corporate, or promotional use. eBook versions and licenses are also available for most titles. For more information, reference our Special Bulk Sales–eBook Licensing web page at www.apress.com/bulk-sales.

Any source code or other supplementary material referenced by the author in this text is available to readers at www.apress.com. For detailed information about how to locate your book's source code, go to www.apress.com/source-code/.

To Amy

Contents at a Glance

Contents

Contents

About the Author

Ed Crookshanks has over 18 years of experience in software development. He started with C on a VAX machine for medical research, moved on to C++ on both Unix and PC platforms, database programming, and finally added some Java and .NET in a wide variety of business domains.

For over nine years Mr. Crookshanks has worked in the financial services industry using .NET, Java, Oracle, SQL Server, Tibco, and many other tools to support line-of-business efforts and procedures. This included web and desktop applications, service applications, and batch processing utilities utilizing FTP, MQ, and web service communication.

He is also a former adjunct professor and a Certified Trainer delivering classes on SQL Server and Visual Studio. He has instructed and performed development on diverse platforms in addition to Microsoft including Java and Java Servlets, PHP, Apache, Tomcat, Android, and Objective-C programming for the iPhone. Active in the local development community, he participates and occasionally presents to the local developer's guild.

Acknowledgments

A book is rarely the work of a single person. One person may be at the keyboard typing everything but there are many other aspects required to complete a book. I hope I don't forget anyone...

First of all, a tremendous thanks to my wife and children for their patience and understanding. Unfortunately books don't type themselves and this necessarily means that other areas can sometimes be neglected. For that I'm sorry.

Thanks to those who have provided input, reviewed, or otherwise given material and moral support throughout this process: Dr. Bill Pierson, Dr. Wahjudi Paulus, Mr. John Biros, Mr. Alberto Botero, Bill Jones Jr., Chris Laforet, and Roy Schilling. A special thanks also to Dr. Venkat Gudivada and the students of his fall 2011 Senior Projects class for their input.

For reading the first edition and providing grammar corrections and other suggestions, I must thank Tom Wessel.

Thanks also to Dorothy Dodenhoff for suggesting and reviewing the section on SQL.

And finally, thanks to Roy Lee Cooke—for the coffee, stories, and inspiration.

Introduction

Purpose

The purpose of this book is to discuss and provide additional resources for topics and technologies that current university curriculums may leave out. Some programs or professors may touch on some of these topics as part of a class, but individually they are mostly not worthy of a dedicated class, and collectively they encompass some of the tools and practices that should be used throughout a software developer's career. Use of these tools and topics is not mandatory, but applying them will give the student a better understanding of the practical side of software development.

In addition, several of these tools and topics are the 'extra' goodies that employers look for experience working with or having a basic understanding of. In discussions with industry hiring managers and technology recruiters, the author has been told repeatedly that fresh college graduates, while having the theoretical knowledge to be hired, are often lacking in more practical areas such as version control systems, unit testing skills, debugging techniques, interpreting business requirements, and others. This is not to slight or degrade institutional instruction, only to point out that there are tools and techniques that are part of enterprise software development that don't fit well within the confines of an educational environment. Knowledge of these can give the reader an advantage over those who are unfamiliar with them.

This guide will discuss those topics and more in an attempt to fill in the practical gaps. In some cases the topics are code-heavy, in other cases the discussion is largely a survey of methods or a discussion of theory. Students who have followed this guide should have the means to talk intelligently on these topics and this will hopefully translate to an advantage in the area of job hunting. While it would be impossible to cover all tools and technologies, the ones covered in this guide are a good representative sample of what is used in the industry today. Beyond the theoretical aspects of computer science are the practical aspects of the actual implementation; it is this realm that this book attempts to de-mystify.

In short, it is hoped that this companion guide will help graduates overcome the "lack of practical experience" issue by becoming more familiar with industry standard practices and common tools. This volume we cannot create experts but it can at least provide enough cursory knowledge such that the reader can discuss the basics of each topic during an interview. With a little practice and exploration on their own, the student should realize that supplementing an excellent theoretical education with practical techniques will hopefully prove useful not only in writing better software while in school, but also translate to an advantage when out of school and searching for a job.

Overview of Topics

The following topics and tools are discussed:

- Version control

- Unit Testing and Test Driven Development

- Refactoring

- Build tools, automated build engineering, and continuous integration

- Debugging

- Comparison of development methodologies

- Design patterns and architecture

- Requirements

- Basic SQL statements and data frameworks

Prerequisites

It is assumed the reader is already familiar with many facets of languages and tools. The typical student would have used Java, .NET, C++, or some other high-level language for course assignments in a typical computer science or software curriculum and is probably at the sophomore, junior, or senior level. The reader should also be familiar with the differences between console applications, GUI applications, and service/daemon applications. The nuances of procedural, object-oriented, and event-driven program should be known at a high-level if not better. The examples will be kept as simple as possible where needed because the intent is not to teach CS topics and object-oriented design, but how to use these particular tools and concepts to assist in implementing the problem at hand.

Disclaimer

The tools and techniques discussed in this guide are not the only ones on the market. If a particular tool is mentioned in this guide it does not mean that it is the only tool for the job, is endorsed in any way by the author or publisher, or is superior in any way to any of its competitors. Nor does mention of any tool in this publication insinuate in any way that the tool owners or resellers support or endorse this work.

Java and Java-based trademarks are the property of Sun Microsystems. Visual Studio® is a registered product of Microsoft and all other Microsoft product trademarks, registered products, symbols, logos, and other intellectual property is listed at http://www.microsoft.com/about/legal/en/us/IntellectualProperty/Trademarks/EN-US.aspx. Eclipse™ is property of the Eclipse Foundation. All other trademarks, registered trademarks, logos, patents, and registered names are the property of their respective owner(s). We are aware of these ownership claims and respect them in the remainder of the text by capitalizing or using all caps when referring to the tool or company in the text.

Any example code is not warranted and the author cannot be held liable for any issues arising from its use. Also, the references provided for each topic are most definitely not an exhaustive list and again, their mention is not to be construed as an endorsement, nor is any resource left off the list to be considered unworthy. Many additional books, web sites, and blogs are available on these topics and should be investigated for alternate discussions. Any mentions of names anywhere in the book are works of fiction and shouldn't be associated with any real person.

Software Notes

Examples are provided in a variety of languages and with different tools, all of which have some level of free software available. Enterprise versions of these tools may exist, or similar tools with stricter licensing models and slightly different semantics may exist; it is simply assumed that tools at the educational level will be closer to the free versions. Also, most hobby developers or recent graduates will probably make use of free tools instead of starting with an expensive development tool suite. If a particular topic/example is not given in a familiar language or with a familiar tool it should be easily translated into another environment. Where possible, notes on how different platforms solve different problems in different ways will be noted. Some of these tools may already be mandated by an employer, others may be free to choose which tools to use to start a practice discussed here. The development tools are the current release available in early 2011, namely Visual Studio 2010 Express Editions, and Eclipse 3.6. Other tools used in the text were obtained around the same time.

Please note—the examples will be kept necessarily simple. In fact, most of the examples will be so short that the tools and techniques used on them will probably not seem worth it. However, in the context of much larger systems, enterprise systems, these tools and techniques are very useful.

■ ■ ■

CHAPTER 1

Version Control

Version control, sometimes referred to as the code or source repository, can serve several purposes in a typical software development organization:

1. To coordinate project source code between different developers or groups of developers.

2. To serve as the 'system of record' for code that goes into production.

3. Centralizing source storage and providing autonomy from developer's machines.

4. Allow for automated tests and builds to occur on demand or at configured times.

In this section we'll first discuss some terminology associated with version control then move on to a technical example.

Theory

The main purpose of any version control system is to attempt to coordinate file sharing amongst multiple developers. For example, if two users want to edit the same source code file, how is that managed? In practice there are two principal modes of operation for source repositories to manage this operation. These two modes can go by many names, but we refer to them in this manual as "Lock on check out" (LOCO) and "Merge on modify" (MOM). These two methods of operation describe how the user interacts with their local copy and how that relates to the same file maintained in the repository.

Many version control tools use the LOCO methodology to address file sharing issues. In this method, when a user requests a file from the central repository, it is unavailable, or "locked" to all other users who request it. This is known as "checking out" the file and the analogy is similar to a library book. Only in the case of version control an unedited copy still exists in the repository while the user has a "working copy" they can edit. In this way the user can make changes to their local copy and constantly compare their modifications to the unedited copy in the repository. Until the user who is editing the file "checks it in" to the repository no one else can edit the file. This is a method of "forced serialization" – one user editing a file will lock *all* other users from editing that file until the file is checked in.

A different approach is the MOM method. Is this method, multiple users can get a working copy of the source file from the repository. Each user then makes changes to their local "working copy" in the course of their normal work. When the users then "check in" their local copies, the system has built in logic to smoothly merge the changes into a single file. Although this seems as if it would be more chaotic than the LOCO method, it is rare that two users are editing the same place in the same file at the same time. If so, the version control system can detect this and signal a conflict which must be resolved manually. In practice this rarely happens, and when it does it forces communication between the two (or more) team members. In addition, since multiple members can edit the same file at the same time there is no waiting for someone to check in a file.

In the technical section below, both Ron and Nancy get a copy of the source files. At this point there is an unrevised copy of each file in the repository, and both Ron and Nancy have local working copies that they each can modify. If Ron gets done quickly and checks his file back in, the repository now contains the updated version and Nancy still has the original file with her changes only. Later, when she attempts to check her file back in, the system will let her know that there has been changes to the repository version since her last check out. At that point, she must request an update from the repository. The version control system will bring a fresh copy from the repository and attempt to merge the repository version (with Ron's changes) into her local working copy. If all goes well she will end up with a file that contains both her changes and Ron's changes. She can now recompile locally and test out both her changes and Ron's changes for programming conflicts. If none are found she can now check in her version to the repository. After Nancy's check in the repository will contain both of their changes. Ron will have to update his file to get the changes done by Nancy.

Software Demonstration

Most version control systems have at least 3 types of client tools: shell commands, GUI clients, and IDE plug-ins. In this book we won't cover the shell commands but will look at two types of plug-in components.

For the first software demonstration we will use Subversion and the Tortoise SVN plug-in for the Microsoft Windows File Explorer. Subversion (also referred to as "svn") is very popular but there are many other vendors of version control software in the market. Others include ClearCase from IBM, Visual SourceSafe from Microsoft, Microsoft Team System, CVS, and Git.

In this demonstration some liberties will be taken for illustrative purposes. All files and the repository will be local to one machine, but it will be pointed out where the process would differ for a remote server. Also, instead of different users, multiple directories will be used to simulate different users.

First, we need some source code to control. A bare-bones C# Windows Forms application was created with Visual Studio 2010 Express Edition. The logic of the application simply says "Hello" to the user when the "Say Hello" button is pushed. The file structure is shown below:

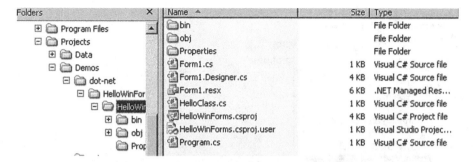

Figure 1-1. Example Project Files

Visually we can tell that the code is not under SVN control because the icons appear normal. After we put the code under version control the icons will be decorated with a sprite that will give us a visual clue as to the file's status.

First we need to install the Tortoise SVN tool. This is simply a download from tortoise svn site: http://tortoisesvn.tigris.org/. After installing with the default settings there will be a menu item for "TortoiseSVN". If you try to run the TortoiseSVN program you will get a warning message that this is a snap in and can't be run as a separate program. This warning is shown below:

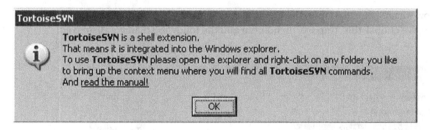

Figure 1-2. Warning that Tortoise is a plug-in

So if we return to our explorer window, we now have an additional context menu when right-clicking on a folder, shown in Figure 1-3. FOR THIS LOCAL DEMONSTRATION ONLY we will first create a local repository. It is usually the responsibility of a separate person or team to manage the repository, so a developer would rarely be tasked with creating an actual repository. To do this locally, we navigate in explorer to our directory that will act as our repository, right click on the folder and from the SVN context menu choose "Create repository here." This location will then become the "URL" of our repository and is discussed in more detail a little later when actually importing the code. Note that this is not our project location but a complete separate folder. From Figure 1-4 it can be seen that the repository location in this instance is "C:\Utils\SNV_Repo" and not our project directory. But just to reiterate; in a typical scenario a manager or even a completely separate team would create a repository, and the URL would be an intranet address, not a local file path.

Figure 1-3. *Context menu for TortoiseSVN*

Now we are going to Import the files into the repository. Navigating back to our project location, we choose the "Import" menu item and the following dialog is displayed:

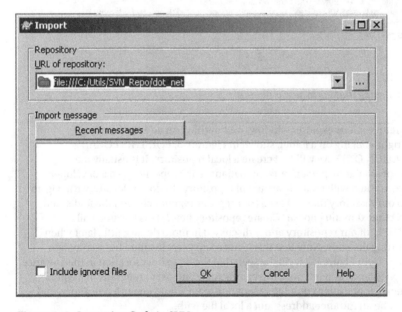

Figure 1-4. *Importing Code in SVN*

Note that in this case, as mentioned above, the URL of the repository is the local file system. THIS IS FOR DEMONSTRATION PURPOSES ONLY. In a typical distributed scenario this would be a URL of an intranet address. The "Import message" field is for annotating the files with a descriptive summary such as "Initial source code check-in." When complete a dialog with a summary of the actions is shown as in Figure 1-5.

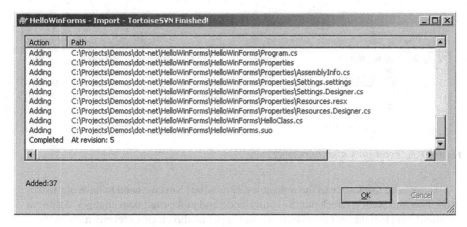

Figure 1-5. *Summary dialog for importing file*

An important piece of information is available in the below summary; "Revision 5" is the unique revision number of the code in the repository. Soon, when we check out the code, we have the ability to ask for the latest version of the code (known as HEAD), or we can ask for a specific revision. This is a neat feature of version control that allows us to "go back in time" and check out code from a previous revision. This could be useful for fixing bugs, performance testing, or simply seeing what changes were made since a certain time in the past. Viewing historical annotations and retrieving a previous version of a file is discussed in more detail later on.

■ **Note** Revision numbers may be handled differently by other version control products. In SVN, the revision identifies the version of the entire project tree. In other products, such as CVS, revision numbers can be applied directly to individual files. Please be sure and read the documentation for whichever product you use.

Note that for this example, I have chosen to import the entire tree, which includes the compiled executable and/or dll files. We will discuss the impact of this a little later on. This policy can differ per organization however; with some including *only* source files and resource files and not the executable. This philosophy stems from the belief that the repository is only for code, not the compiled application itself.

Versioning logic is also what gives us the ability to "Branch" and "Tag" source code, which we discuss later on. In short, branching allows for two different streams of code to co-exists, and tagging is used to further identify a revision of code.

Now if from the context menu we choose to "Browse Repository" there should be a structure like the following figure:

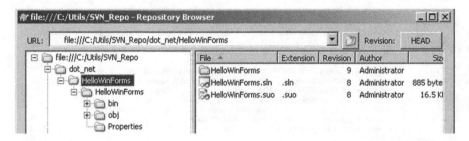

Figure 1-6. *Repository after importing code*

So we have the source in the repository. Now what? Next we need to have our two users, Ron and Nancy, check out the source code and make their own changes. Again, we are simulating two distinct users by using two separate directories, cleverly named "Ron" and "Nancy".

For TortoiseSVN, we navigate to the folder we want to contain our local working copy of the code, right-click, and from the context menu choose "SVN Checkout...", which brings up the dialog box shown in Figure 1-7. Again, the URL in our case is for a local repository. The checkout directory defaults to the one we right-clicked on, and Checkout Depth gives us several options for handling the recursion of the file structure we want to get. Notice also that we have the ability to get the "HEAD" revision or a particular revision number. Using the "Show log" button will bring up a screen for showing revision details such as dates, actions, and messages.

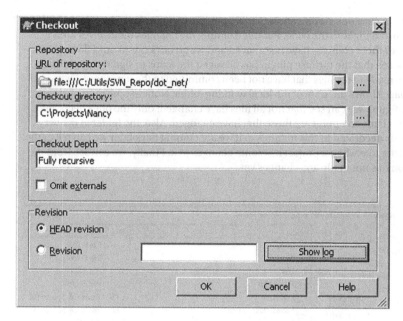

Figure 1-7. *SVN Checkout Command Options*

Since we chose "Fully Recursive" the entire tree is replicated in our local working folder and the folders and files are decorated with special icons. In addition, a special ".svn" folder is added to the directory tree. This is used be the server and SHOULD NOT be modified. The snapshot of the file structure in Figure 1-8 illustrates both directories (Ron and Nancy) after both have checked out the code.

Address	C:\Projects\Nancy\HelloWinForms\HelloWinForms		

Folders	×	Name ▲	Size	Type
☐ 🗀 Nancy		🗀 .svn		File Folder
⊞ 🗀 .svn		🗀 bin		File Folder
☐ 🗀 HelloWinForn		🗀 obj		File Folder
⊞ 🗀 .svn		🗀 Properties		File Folder
☐ 🗀 HelloWin		Form1.cs	1 KB	Visual C# Source file
⊞ 🗀 .svn		Form1.Designer.cs	4 KB	Visual C# Source file
⊞ 🗀 bin		Form1.resx	6 KB	.NET Managed Res…
⊞ 🗀 obj		HelloClass.cs	1 KB	Visual C# Source file
🗀 Prop		HelloWinForms.csproj	4 KB	Visual C# Project file
☐ 🗀 Ron		HelloWinForms.csproj.user	1 KB	Visual Studio Projec…
⊞ 🗀 .svn		Program.cs	1 KB	Visual C# Source file
☐ 🗀 HelloWinForn				
⊞ 🗀 .svn				
⊞ 🗀 HelloWin				

Figure 1-8. *File Structure with decorated icons*

Now we can start our modifications. We'll open the solution from the "Nancy" folder and make some changes to the code. For this example the changes themselves aren't important. After these changes have been saved and we go back out to our File Explorer, we can clearly see that the tortoise plugin has changed the icons to signal that we have some changes made to the files that have not been committed to the repository. Figure 1-9 on the next page shows the state of the local working folder. Notice some of important points in this figure. We can see that not all files have changed; only the ones decorated with the red exclamation point are those that have changed. Also, the folder at the very top of the tree is decorated in this manner so if we are coming back later we can tell at the 'root' level of the tree when a project has some changes to it. Finally, we can see from the figure that Ron has not made any changes yet.

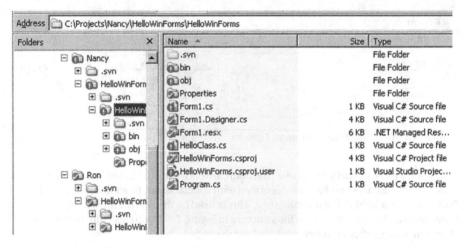

Figure 1-9. *Local files after Nancy's changes*

So let's open the project from the "Ron" folder and make some code changes. Again, the details of the changes are not important, only that we have two different working folders and both working folders have changed code in them. The picture in Figure 1-10 shows the state of the file system after changes to Ron's folder.

Address	C:\Projects\Ron\HelloWinForms		
Folders	**Name** ▲	**Size**	**Type**
⊞ Nancy	.svn		File Folder
⊟ Ron	HelloWinForms		File Folder
⊞ .svn	HelloWinForms.sln	1 KB	Microsoft Visual Stu...
⊟ HelloWinForm	HelloWinForms.suo	18 KB	Visual Studio Solutio...
⊞ .svn			
⊞ HelloWinl			

Figure 1-10. *After Ron's changes*

So now we begin to check in source files and see what happens. First, "Ron" checks in his files. This can either be done one file at a time, by highlighting each file and choosing "SVN Commit...". While this might be desirable in some circumstances, here we will make use of the recursive nature of the system and make that choice on the "Ron" folder. Once we make the section the dialog shown in Figure 1-11 appears. Here we can enter our message for this revision ("Ron's changes to the Winforms app") and if needed we can deselect files that we don't want to check in. In this example we've chosen only the modified source files. One neat feature is the ability to see the difference between the working file and the repository file. As it says in the "Changes made" section, double clicking on a filename will launch an application called Winmerge to see the differences in the local file and the repository. We will talk more about that in a little while. But for now, simply choosing the files to check in, typing a message, and clicking "OK" is all that needs done.

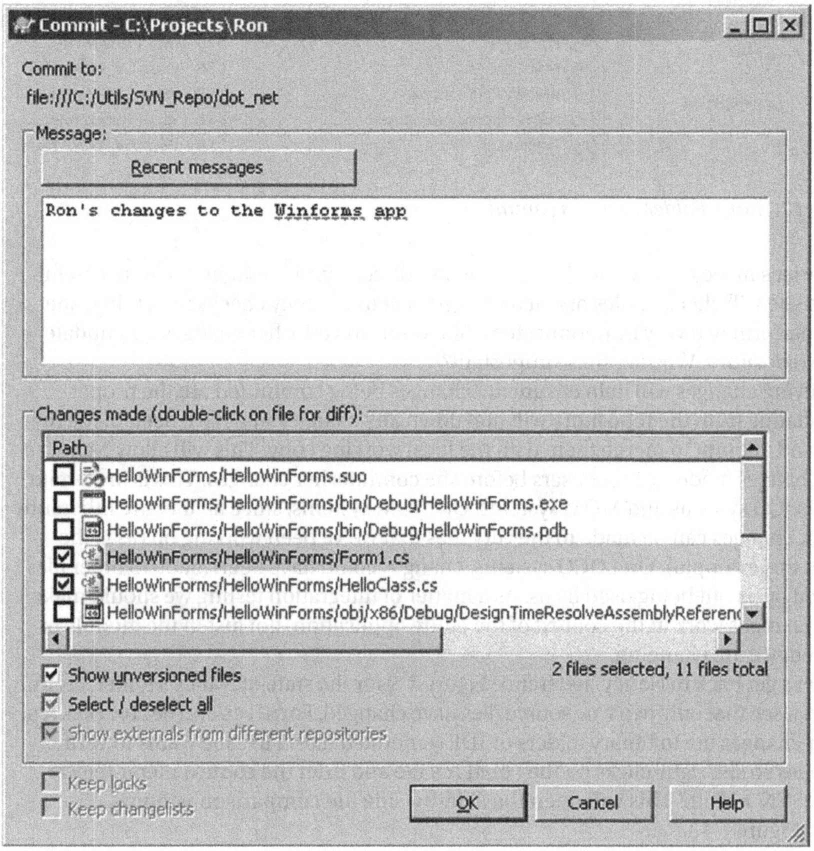

Figure 1-11. SVN Commit options screen

Once the files are checked in we get a summary dialog, similar to the summary dialog when importing files shown in Figure 1-5. Ron's folder will finally look like Figure 1-12. Note that we are beginning to see the downside of our choice to put all files, even binary and IDE-generated files, in version control. Ron's code changes have been completely checked in but his "root" folder, "Ron", still shows the red exclamation point of a folder with changes. We'll discuss more about this a little later.

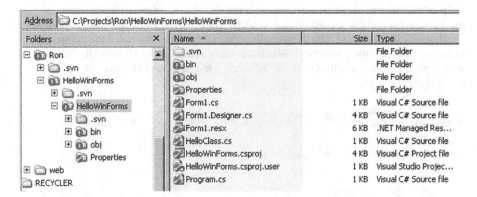

Figure 1-12. *Ron's Folder after his commit*

Now let's move back to the "Nancy" and her directory. Since Nancy is more careful than Ron she will check in files one at a time. Also before Nancy checks in her files, she plans to perform two very important steps. She wants to verify her changes and update from the repository. Why are these important?

Verifying changes will help ensure the changes being committed are the proper ones. Updating from the repository will pull down any changes that have been made in the files and attempt to merge them with the local working copy. This will allow Nancy to see any changes made by other users before she commits her changes. This is important both on LOCO systems and MOM systems. On MOM systems, since all files are inherently unlocked, changes can be made to the very files that we've been working on (as is the case with this example). On LOCO systems, changes could have been made to other files not locked by us but being used by us. As a matter of integration testing we should make sure our changes work in the context of the entire application, not just in the module or component we are changing.

So let's get back to Nancy. Reference Figure 1-9 for the state of Nancy's folder. From that we can see that only two true source files have changed, Form1.cs and HelloClass.cs; the other changes are to binary folders or IDE-generated files. First she wants to verify her changes so she right-clicks on the Form1.cs file and from the context menu selects "TortoiseSVN ➤ Diff." This will open the side-by-side file comparison window, shown in Figure 1-13.

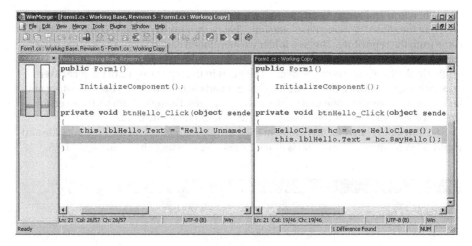

Figure 1-13. *Diff compare before committing*

Again, this is a very simple example and her changes are minor; the important concept is verifying code changes before committing. She is satisfied with this comparison, so she closes this application, right-clicks and chooses "SVN Commit..." and follows the same process as Ron. However in her rush, she forgot to do a "SVN Update" before committing. The result is shown in Figure 1-14.

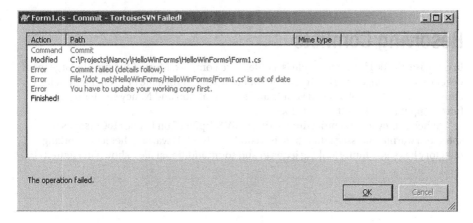

Figure 1-14. *Attempt to commit when working base is old*

When committing, the version control system is smart enough to make sure that her "Working Base" copy is the same as the latest revision in the repository. So this is more than just a "best practice", the repository actually enforces this rule. Confused? Here is a textual explanation of what just happened.

When Ron and Nancy each got their copies of the code from the repository, they both had the same "Working Base" version. That is, they both had exact copies of what came from the repository. The .svn folder we mentioned earlier keeps track of each user's "base" version. This base version is not updated until the user requests it to be. More explicitly, the local copy is not notified of changes in the repository until the local user asks for an update. Once Ron made his changes and checked them in, the repository now had a new base version; one that contained his changes. However Nancy's base version was still the original she received when she first checked out the code.

So how does Nancy fix this problem? She simply right-clicks on the Form1.cs file and chooses "SVN Update." Once that is done she gets the message shown in Figure 1-15.

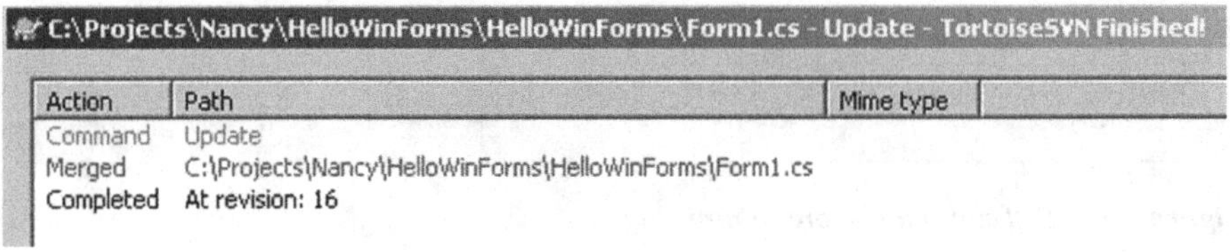

Figure 1-15. *Success Update from the repository*

Now that she has successfully updated *from* the repository, she is free to commit her changes *to* the repository. After committing Form1.cs she follows the same process with HelloClass.cs. Once this is complete the repository will contain changes from both Ron and Nancy.

Resolving Conflicts

In our case, the HelloClass.cs file is a little more complex. Most of the time in large team development changes will be isolated to different sections of a file or even different files altogether. This example was so simple and small that Ron and Nancy can hardly keep from stepping on each other code toes.

When Nancy follows procedure to do an "SVN Update" on her HelloClass.cs file, she gets a warning message that there is a conflict. After this warning her local working directory has some funny looking icons in and some additional files, shown in Figure 1-16.

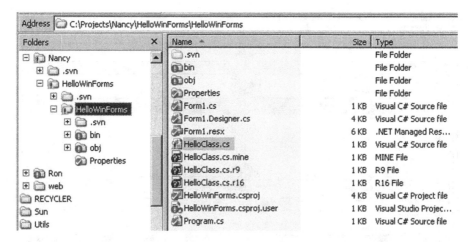

Figure 1-16. *Nancy has a conflict*

To fix this conflict, Nancy right-clicks on the `HelloClass.cs` file and from the context menu chooses "TortoiseSVN ➤ Edit Conflicts" opening the TortoiseMerge screen. Although this screen looks rather busy (and colorful!) it clearly separates Nancy's changes ("Mine") from the repository file ("Theirs") and the attempt at merging them done by the system ("Merged"). The following figures show Nancy's process of merging the changes into a single file.

First, by right-clicking on a conflict line, a context menu with choices of where to pull the resolved source from is shown. Nancy makes her choices, maybe having to consult with Ron while doing so. The final version of her resolution, shown in Figure 1-19, contains both her and Ron's changes. Once this is complete Nancy can save the merged file and mark the conflict as resolved by choosing "Edit ➤ Mark as Resolved" from the menu. Nancy's local directory will now look normal, as shown in Figure 1-20.

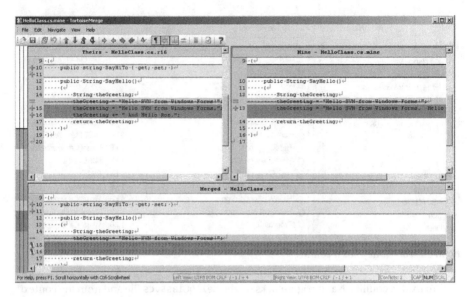

Figure 1-17. *Original merge screen*

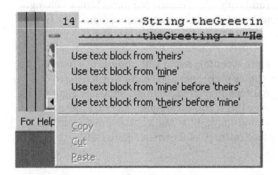

Figure 1-18. *Context menu for a conflict line*

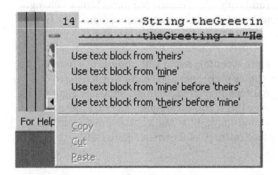

Figure 1-19. *Manually merged file results*

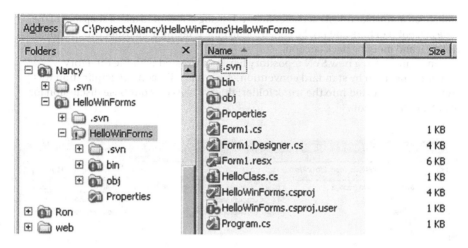

Figure 1-20. *After conflict resolution*

Although she has resolved the conflict, she still has to commit her changes. This is a simple matter of following the normal commit procedure and should work smoothly now that see has merged her changes with the repository.

So our repository now contains both Ron's and Nancy's changes, but there is one final issue to discuss; that of Ron's local working source status. Although he doesn't need Nancy's changes to make his code work correctly, he doesn't want to make new changes to stale source code either. Not only could that make his life miserable by having several conflicts when committing, he could potentially miss changes that are an important prerequisite to his changes. So as a best practice, one should always perform an update before modifying any code. That goes for both LOCO and MOM systems.

Tagging and Branching

Keeping track of changes and allowing for concurrent editing is an important feature of version control. But other important capabilities exist as well. Tagging (or labeling) provides a mechanism to identify a particular revision of code as important, say for a particular milestone in the development process or at a release point.

Branching allows some code to be isolated into a separate area. That area can be worked on independently without disturbing the main line of code. When the "branch" is complete it can be merged back into the main line. The main line is often referred to as the "trunk."

Different tools handle these concepts in different ways. Some apply tags directly to source files and allow for simply retrieving all files based on a tag. SVN has a convention of creating a directory structure with a separate folder for tags.

Branching is also handled in different ways; sometimes it is even transparent to the developer if retrieving and editing a previous version of a file. In those instances, when a previous version of a file is retrieved, a branch is created and later can be merged with the main trunk. In SVN a folder convention is followed, similar to tags. In fact, tagging and branch are almost identical except for intent. Tagging is meant to take a snapshot of the code at a point in time and not be edited; branching is taking a snapshot with the intent of editing it and merging back later on.

In Figure 1-21, a new SVN repository has been created with the directory structure specified by standard convention. A simple .NET console application was created and imported into the trunk folder; this will serve as our base discussion for the rest of the section.

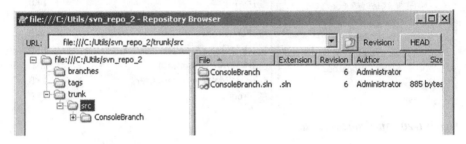

Figure 1-21. *SVN Repository with structure*

To begin with we will tag our existing code as the base version. In a simple project like this identifying the file that makes of the base version is quite easy, but in a larger project with several files and/or projects within a solution it could be much more difficult. Also, in the content of many developers and many revision numbers it may be much harder to remember – was the release of revision number 181 or 183?

To create a tag in the repository, Tortoise is used. After checking out the project and making sure that it compiles and runs as expected, we right-click on the project folder and select "Branch/tag" from the context menu, shown in Figure 1-22. The "Copy (Branch/Tag)" dialog box appears as captured in Figure 1-23. Using this dialog allows us create both tags and branches; the difference being in the "To URL:" specification. The screen capture shows that the destination is "/tags/base-version" in our repository; hence here are creating a tag. Also note that there are a couple of other options the operation. The tag could be applied to a specific revision in the repository so tags/branches can be done "after the fact." Another option is to use the current working copy. This would be done for example if there were significant changes done to the local working copy that can't be discarded but for some reason cannot be checked in.

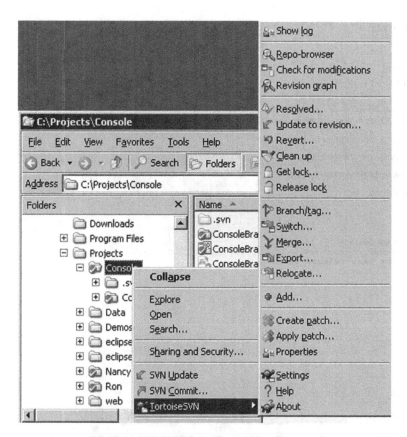

Figure 1-22. *Branch/tag in the context menu*

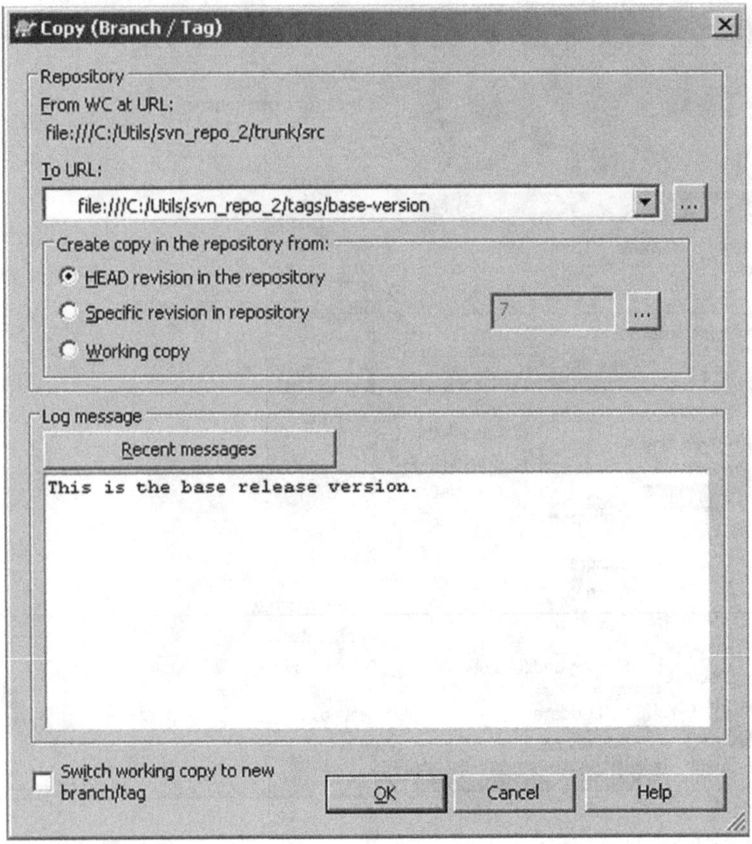

Figure 1-23. *Branch/tag dialog box*

Clicking "OK" will create the tag. If the checkbox "Switch working copy to new branch/tag" is checked the working copy will be switched to the branch or tag; in this case that isn't necessary because the working copy and the tag are one and the same. The "base copy" is to remain unchanged so not switching to that tag is the desired behavior. The completion dialog for the creation reiterates that as well, shown in Figure 1-24

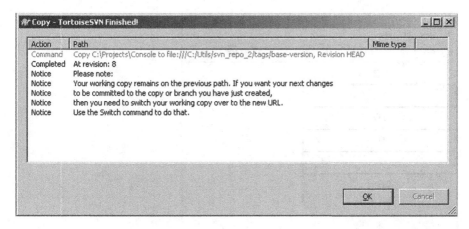

Figure 1-24. *Result of creating a tag*

In SVN, branching works in the same fashion as tagging except for the "To URL:" specification. Right-clicking on the folder, choosing "Branch/tag" and specifying a sub-folder in the "branches" folder for the "To URL:" will result in a new branch being created. In the case of a branch the developer may indeed want to switch directly to the branch so that editing occurs in the branch and not the trunk.

To illustrate this, minor modifications will be made to the console application's main file merely to increase the revision number in the trunk folder. After several revisions a branch will be created and edited separately. Then the branch and the trunk will be merged. Finally, in the next section these revisions will be examined and it will be shown how to retrieve a specific tag and revision.

The simple modifications made to the Main() method are shown below. Indeed, they are quite simple but will be used to clearly illustrate the branching and merging process.

To see the history and revisions in SVN, the item from the SVN menu (shown in Figure 1-22) to choose is "Revision Graph." The result of the revision graph on the Program.cs file is shown in Figure 1-25.

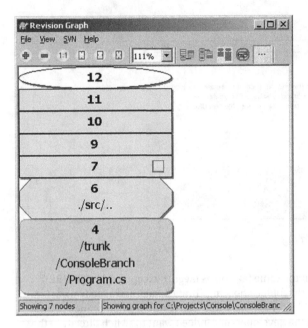

Figure 1-25. Revision History

Listing 1-1. Modifed Main Method

```
static void Main(string[] args)
{
    Console.WriteLine("This will be a branching and merging app...");
    Console.WriteLine("This is the base version.");
    Console.WriteLine("This is after the 1st modification");
    Console.WriteLine("This is after the 2nd modification");
    Console.WriteLine("This is after the 3rd modification in TRUNK");
    Console.WriteLine("The final modification in TRUNK.");
    String c;
    Console.WriteLine("Press <enter> to end...");
    c = Console.ReadLine();
}
```

From the revision graph a good idea of what has happened to the file can be seen. Although explaining all of the shapes and symbols will not be done here, a few are worth noting. Starting from the bottom:

- This particular file was added to the repository at revision 4

- The file was moved in to the /src/ directory resulting in revision 6

- Revision 7 has a tag applied (this was the tag applied earlier in this section)

- Several revisions of the file have been checked into the repository (9, 10, 11, and 12)

- The latest version is revision 12

If you're asking the question of why does revision 7 of the file have the tag, but the dialog in Figure 1-24 talks about revision 8, the explanation is simple. Recall that in SVN every modification to the repository increments the revision number. Since a tag is essentially a copy of the repository at a specific point this is indeed a modification. Hence the tagged file is at revision 7, but the tag is actually revision 8.

Before creating the branch, first recall the structure of the repository. As shown below in Figure 1-26, the repository has three folders – trunk, tags, and branches. This is a fairly standard convention but is not enforced by SVN. However it does clearly illustrate the structure of the repository clearly. Note also that the tag "base-version" has a revision number of 8, as discussed on the previous page.

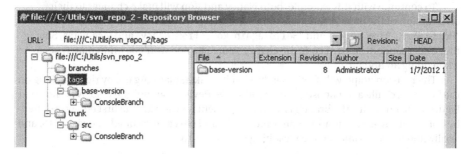

Figure 1-26. *Repository Structure*

Following the same logic as that for a tag, a branch will be created by using Tortoise plug-in and choosing "Brach/Tag" as shown in Figure 1-22. However instead of the "To URL:" field referring to a folder under the "tags" folder, a folder under the "branches" folder is specified. To get highly creative this will be called "branches/my-first-branch" and when complete the repository will look like Figure 1-27. Notice the branch is revision 13 even though the latest file was revision 12. A branch, like a tag, will increment the revision because the repository changes.

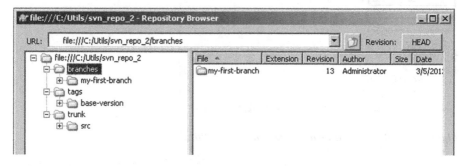

Figure 1-27. *Repository after branching*

Recall that there is the option to "Switch working copy to new branch/tag" but for illustrative purposes that will not be chosen here. We will simulate completely separate users checking working on two lines of code.

Remember Ron and Nancy from earlier? They are at it again. This time Nancy will be working on the "trunk" code while Ron makes changes to the "my-first-branch" branch of code.

Since Nancy's checkout is from the trunk line of code, her process is similar to that surrounding Figure 1-7, the only difference being the name of the project and location in the repository she is checking out code from; in this case the URL for checkout would be the file:///C:/Utils/svn_repo_2/trunk/src location.

Ron's checkout is from the branch line of code, so he too checks out code from the same repository; however the URL he uses is file:///C:/Utils/svn_repo_2/branches/ my-first-branch which gets him the code from a different place than Nancy. At this point the two code lines are exactly the same, but in a live environment these may be an infrequent occurrence.

To continue with this example, both Nancy and Ron will make changes to their own version of the Main() function shown in Listing 1.1 by adding statements such as "Hello Ron, from Nancy" and "Hello again Ron, from Nancy" and vice-versa. Since they are in separate lines of code the changes made by one won't be immediately seen when doing an update.

The revision graph will show exactly what has taken place. Again, by right-clicking on the Program.cs file and choosing "TortoiseSVN ➤ Revision graph" the display is shown in Figure 1-28. From this the branch is seen to represent revision 13; the first edit was done by Ron resulting in revision 14; then Nancy's edit and check-in resulted in revision 15; and finally Ron made another change resulting in revision 16.

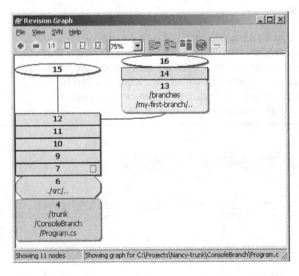

Figure 1-28. *Revision graph after branching and editing*

Again, notice how the revision numbers are not linear "per branch", meaning that Nancy's version goes from 12 to 15. This is simply a function of the way SVN works. Other version control systems may version individual files instead of the repository as a whole, but the principal remains the same.

Now it is time to merge the branch back into the main trunk line of code. Given that only one file has been edited this single file could be merged back, but in this case the entire project will be merged. Again, each project will be different with many different scenarios but the overall process is similar.

For this example, Nancy will right-click on her project root directory and choose "TortoiseSVN ➤ Merge" which will start a Merge wizard. The first page of the wizard is for choosing a "Merge Type", each of which has a fairly detailed description of how it is to be used. This is shown in Figure 1-29.

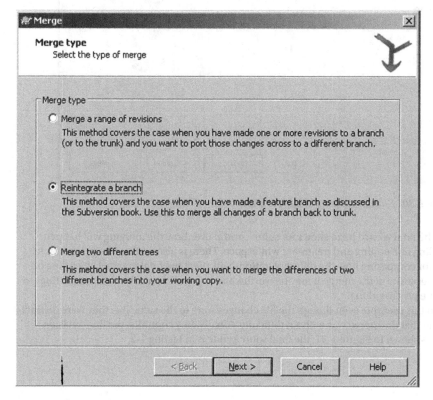

Figure 1-29. *Selecting a Merge type*

The second page of the wizard is for specifying the locations. Note that for reintegrating a branch the only thing to specify is the branch where the code is coming from, as shown in Figure 1-30. The other options have very different options as range of revision numbers or two separate branches may have to be specified.

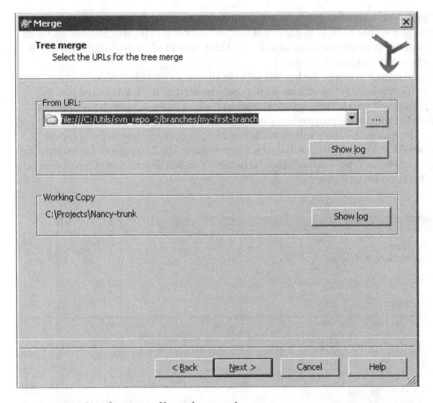

Figure 1-30. Simple merge of branch to trunk

The final wizard page allows for some control over how the merging will happen regarding line ending and treatment whitespace. There is also a "Test Merge" button to allow for comparing how the different options will affect the final merge. Depending on the complexity of the merge it may be worthwhile to experiment with different settings to ease the process along.

In this example even though the file changes were to the same file, they were distinct enough that the merge was without difficulty. After Nancy commits, the final revision graph is shown in Figure 1-31; the final source code is in Listing 1-2.

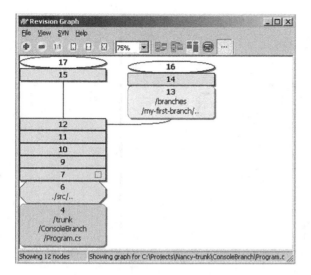

Figure 1-31. *Revision graph after merging branch to trunk*

Listing 1-2. Final source code after merging

```
static void Main(string[] args)
{
    Console.WriteLine("This will be a branching and merging app...");
    Console.WriteLine("This is the base version.");
    Console.WriteLine("This is after the 1st modification");
    Console.WriteLine("This is after the 2nd modification");
    Console.WriteLine("This is after the 3rd modification in TRUNK");
    Console.WriteLine("The final modification in TRUNK.");
    Console.WriteLine("Hi Nancy, this is from Ron.");
    Console.WriteLine("Hi again Nancy, this is from Ron (again).");
    String c;
    Console.WriteLine("Hi Ron, this is from Nancy");
    Console.WriteLine("Press <enter> to end...");
    c = Console.ReadLine();
}
```

Finally, even though the picture in the figure below is from another version control tool, can you guess what situation the following graph represents? The answer is in the discussion appendix for this part.

25

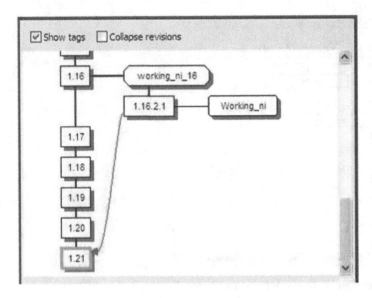

Figure 1-32. What's going on here?

Retrieving a Previous Version

Thus far in the checkout of projects the code has always been retrieved from the latest version, also known as the "head" of the source code graph. There are a number ways to "go back" and get older versions, the two most common will be discussed here.

First of all, if a different version of the project is desired when checking out from the repository, simply specify an earlier version when checking out the code. This will pull the code at that revision level and the working directory will contain will contain code from that time. This can be used to recreate a previous bug to see how it was fixed; or to see how a particular operation was done in the past. Typically older revisions aren't worked on and updated as merging these with the latest version may cause conflicts.

Second, when viewing the revision graph there is an option for "Update WC to revision" which will update the current working copy to the revision desired. Note however that in the case of viewing and or editing a previous version, any time an "update" from the repository is done, the working copy is updated against the latest version in the repository. So the process of checking out an older version and immediately doing an update would be the same as checking out the latest version.

What to keep in the repository

As has been shown in the examples above, it can sometimes lead to confusion if all user files and compiled binary files for a project or solution are kept in the repository. In the above example the changed source was committed but the parent directory still showed changes because both compiled binaries (.exe) and user-specific tool files (.suo) were kept in the repository. Ideally only source code and supporting files, such as solution or project metadata files, third-party libraries (that do not change when developer code is compiled), and configuration files should be kept in the repository. These can be considered "input" files; the "output" files such as JARs, EXEs, or DLLs that are built by compiling the source code should not be stored in the repository. This allows any user or automated build tool to get a copy of the source code (input files) and compile a version of the binary (output files). If the source code is the same, the resultant binary output file(s) should be the same between compiles. These new output files in the workspace will not affect the status of the repository.

To alleviate the problem in the above example, the user and compiled files would need to be removed from the repository and their file extensions added to the "ignore list." This is shown in Figure 1-33; to always exclude .NET user files, the user would choose the "*.suo" choice. After doing this for all user files and other binaries (object files, debug files, etc.) within a project/solution and committing the changes, the version control system will ignore those files going forward.

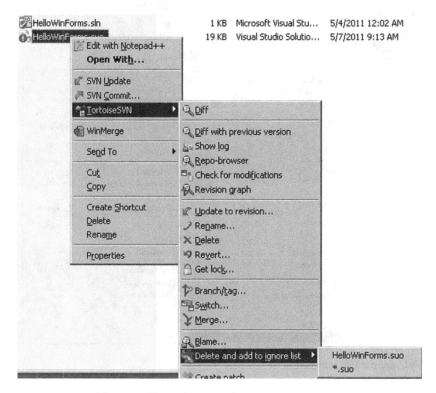

Figure 1-33. *Adding user files to the ignore list*

IDE Integration

Many version control products have integration modules for Integrated Development Environment (IDE) products. For example, a CVS repository plug-in is included by default in the Eclipse IDE. Microsoft has Team System support built in to certain editions of Visual Studio, and plug-ins for other systems, such as CVS, SVN, and of course Visual SourceSafe are available. Unlike the example above these plug-ins allow for all the same operations we discussed with Tortoise, but from directly within the IDE. The snapshot in Figure 1-34 shows an example of the Subversive plug-in accessed from the package explorer menu.

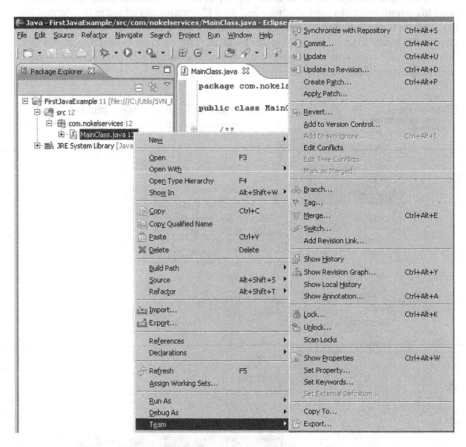

Figure 1-34. *Eclipse IDE integration*

Please note that in this entire discussion some type of GUI tool, either a File Explorer plug-in or a tool integrated into the IDE, has been used. Every command that has been done has an equivalent command-line counterpart; it is simply easier and clearer to show the results and actions at the GUI level. However, depending on the standard practice at a particular software company, command line syntax might be required knowledge. Also note that there may be times when an advanced operation can be done only from the command line. Although beyond the scope of this book, the reader is advised to at least get familiar with the command-line version of the major operations of each tool.

The very simplest operation – checking out a project – is shown below in Figure 1-35. Recall that "file:///c:/Utils/svn_repo_2/truck/src" is the location of the repository; in a real situation this would be the URL of the repository either on the intranet or internet.

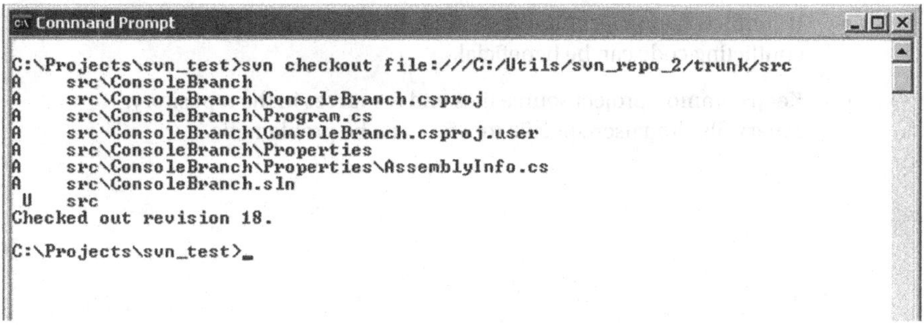

```
C:\Projects\svn_test>svn checkout file:///C:/Utils/svn_repo_2/trunk/src
A    src\ConsoleBranch
A    src\ConsoleBranch\ConsoleBranch.csproj
A    src\ConsoleBranch\Program.cs
A    src\ConsoleBranch\ConsoleBranch.csproj.user
A    src\ConsoleBranch\Properties
A    src\ConsoleBranch\Properties\AssemblyInfo.cs
A    src\ConsoleBranch.sln
 U   src
Checked out revision 18.

C:\Projects\svn_test>_
```

Figure 1-35. Command line checkout

Distributed Version Control

The previous sections discussed version control using SVN, which is a centralized version control system. That is, it has a "central" server and "clients" interact with it and it only. This is very popular in enterprise situations where the infrastructure exists to support a large central system and the connection to the system is consistent and reliable as is the case with an enterprise intranet. In recent years, distributed version controls systems have gained popularity, especially in decentralized situations such as open source development or where small teams are geographically dispersed. Although many of the core concepts are the same (editing a local copy, diff, merge, check-in, etc.), the discussion of distributed teams in Chapter 6 - Development Methodologies and SDLC will further expand on the theory of distributed version control and its different terminology compared to what has been discussed here.

Version Control Summary

In this section we have attempted to give a very brief overview of version control. We discussed theory and usage, and introduced several terms that can carry between systems. We purposely left out topics such as "rolling back" and "abandoning changes." Those topics and more in-depth discussions of what we did cover can be found in any number of additional reference books on version control, some of which are listed in the Appendix.

Although we mainly used SVN and Tortoise there are many tools out there that accomplish these same goals. No matter the tool, we outlined a few steps that should make your life under version control easier:

- Before modifying any code, do a complete update from the repository.

- Before committing any code, also do an update to ensure the latest code from the repository is merged with the local working copy.

- If conflicts happen, communication with the author of the conflicting code can be beneficial.

- Keep common project source files and resources in the repository. Binary files and user-specific tool files can be problematic.

■ ■ ■

CHAPTER 2

Unit Testing and Test Driven Development

Theory

Unit testing refers to being able to repeatedly and reliably test a piece of software – a "unit" - for proper functionality. These tests occur at the developer level to ensure that code written for some desired functionality behaves as expected. By ensuring that each "unit" passes the test(s) that it was designed for, the developer can ensure that as the code is integrated into larger and more complex systems each piece of software remains valid.

Unlike earlier testing strategies, these tests are usually part of the project being tested and can be automated. Getting into the mindset of always running these tests before and after making any changes to the source code may actually lower maintenance and overall testing time because the changes are automatically verified to not affect existing code.

To assist in this endeavor there are numerous supporting tools for most major languages. JUnit is a tool for Java testing; NUnit is a tool for .NET languages. There is even CPPUTest for C++ unit tests. In this section we will describe the basic semantics for JUnit and NUnit and then move into using unit tests for test driven development.

Unit Testing Frameworks

Using a unit testing framework usually involves a separate project in your workspace or solution. The framework provides additional classes and may use decorative attributes, class inheritance and naming conventions to identify tests. The tests are written such that a desired response is checked against an actual response for a specific action. As the class under test grows more tests can be added; thereby eventually testing all code in a component, or unit, of software. We will first start with a single test for a single function, both in Java and .NET, and then expand on that test as we move into our discussion of Test Driven Development.

JUnit

JUnit is the standard unit testing framework for Java development. It is tightly integrated into the Eclipse IDE, so that is what the example will consist of. First, a Java project with a class and method for calculating a food item sales tax will be created. The code for this doesn't get much simpler:

Listing 2-1. Example method to test

```
package companion.UnitTesting;

public class ItemTaxCalc
{
        public static double CalcItemTax(double itemPrice,
            double taxPct)
        {
                double dec = taxPct/10.0;
                return itemPrice * dec;
        }
}
```

So now we need to test this method. Since JUnit is built in to Eclipse, this is pretty easy. We can simply right-click on our ItemTaxCalc.java file, select "New ➤ JUnit Test Case" and the test case creation dialog will appear. This dialog is shown in Figure 2-1.

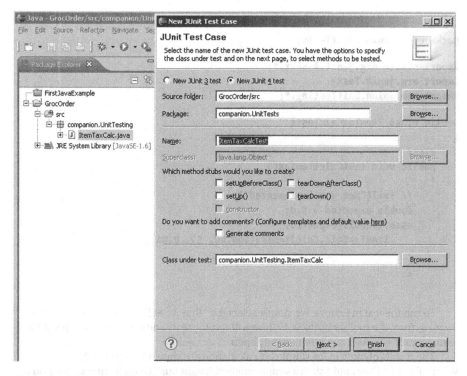

Figure 2-1. *New JUnit Test Case Dialog*

Notice we have the option to generate additional method stubs such as "setUp()" and "tearDown()" but we won't use those in this test. Clicking "next" will allow you to choose which methods to test. This will list all the methods in our class and all base classes as well. For now we choose our new CalcItemTax() method as the only method to test, and press "Finish." Note that if this is our first test we may have to add the JUnit Jar to the build path (Eclipse will do this for us but issue a warning dialog).

The generated code, because we chose the "New JUnit 4 test" option, is decorated with the testing framework's annotation. A "JUnit3 test" instead would have extended the "TestCase" base class. Either way, this class is identified to the run-time as a testable class with a testable method.

We implement our test case; the code is shown in Listing 2-2. Notice that the original stub had the fail("Not Yet Implemented"); as the method body, I've commented that out so the test will pass.

Listing 2-2. Complete test case code

```java
package companion.UnitTests;

import static org.junit.Assert.*;
import org.junit.Test;
import companion.UnitTesting.*;

public class ItemTaxCalcTests
{
    @Test
    public void testCalcItemTax()
    {
        // fail("Not yet implemented");
        double expected = 5.0;
        assertEquals(expected,
            ItemTaxCalc.CalcItemTax(100.00, 5), 0.01);

    }
}
```

To run the test in Eclipse, we simply select the "Run As ➤ JUnit Test" option from the menu or from the toolbar buttons. Eclipse will run the tests and open up a new JUnit View to display the results if one is not already open.

The results of our run for simple tax calculation are shown in Figure 2-2. What!? Failure? How could such a simple method have a bug? Upon further inspection of Listing 2-1 it looks as though we divided wrong – what should have been a divide by 100 was originally coded as divide by 10. Fixing the math error and re-running the test will produce a solid green bar – meaning that our test now passes.

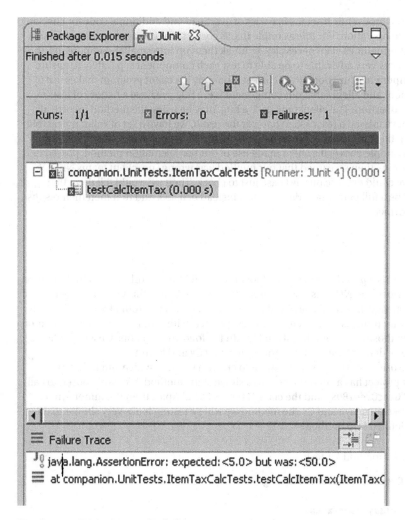

Figure 2-2. *JUnit view and a failing test*

So how is this useful? It seems like a lot of overhead and additional code for checking a simple math operation. For this example that is correct. But in larger systems it is often desired, and sometimes even necessary, to break them up into smaller components. In this scenario it is very advisable to be able to test each component separately to ensure that the component's functionality is correct. That way if a client program makes use of our component and alleges that out component has a bug, we have a battery of tests to back up our assertion. The client may have a bug, may be using the method incorrectly, or we may have missed a test case. Whatever the result, we have a set of valid, repeatable tests that can be automatically run to help prove the results one way or the other. Even the simple example above; if a client made use of our tax calculation method, passed in 0.095 for the rate, then screamed that our method was wrong (no, client teams NEVER do that…) we could execute our test case just to check. Then we would tell them that they should be a full percentage decimal, 9.5, instead of 0.095, and that then their results should be correct.

NUnit

The NUnit tool is a popular unit testing tool for the .NET framework. The main difference in our scenario is that NUnit is a stand-alone tool; at the time of this writing it does not integrate as an add-in with Visual Studio. However since Visual Studio Express allows us to create library projects we can create the test projects within our main software solution and then run those tests from the NUnit GUI. In the following sections we will duplicate the work we've demonstrated above, this time using C# and NUnit.

First we use Visual C# Express Edition to create a solution with a single library project. The project has a single class with a single static method. We have chosen to call the project "GrocOrderBus" and the class "ItemTaxCalc." Apart from the minor syntax differences between Java and C# the method we will be testing looks very similar to the previously defined Java method.

Listing 2-3. C# method for test

```
namespace GrocOrderBus.UnitTesting
{
    public class ItemTaxCalc
    {
        public static double CalcItemTax(
            double itemPrice, double taxPct)
        {
            double dec = taxPct / 10.0;
            return itemPrice * dec;
        }
    }
}
```

So now we need to write our unit test. Again, because NUnit doesn't integrate directly into Visual Studio there is a little more setup than with JUnit and Eclipse. However the end result will be just as informative.

■ **Note**   Higher level editions of Visual Studio have a built-in unit testing framework called the Visual Studio Unit Testing Framework. The syntax is similar in that a separate project is created and classes and methods are decorated with special attributes. A unit testing toolbar is available, as is a separate dockable view window to display the results. With this available one never has to leave the IDE, which some find desirable.

We begin by adding another library project to our solution. We call this project ItemTaxCalcTests. Now our solution has two projects; our project with our class and method to test, and another normal library project which we will turn into our unit test project.

Before we can set up our test we have to import the necessary NUnit library into our new test project. We assume that you have already installed the NUnit tool; that is simply a matter of going to the web site nunit.org, downloading the latest version (or specified version if you need an older version), and then installing either by executing the windows installer package or unzipping the binaries to a location of your choice. Once that is complete you add a reference to the NUnit library in your project. To do this, right-click on the References folder and select Add Reference. This is shown below in Figure 2-3. The nunit.framework.dll assembly will allow us to start annotating our classes and methods to identify them as unit tests. Also, because we have two separate projects, we must "Add Reference" again but this time reference the project ("Projects" tab in Figure 2-3) containing the assembly to test.

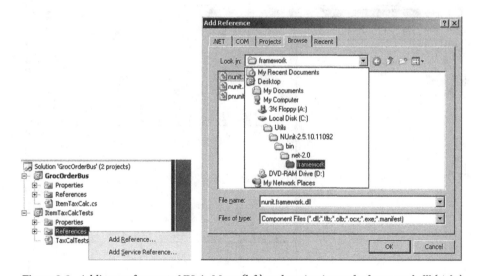

Figure 2-3. Adding a reference to NUnit. Menu (left) and navigating to the framework dll (right)

Our complete testing code is shown in Figure 2-4. Note that the figure also shows the project structure and references of the testing project. Once we build the entire solution we are ready to start executing the test with the NUnit GUI.

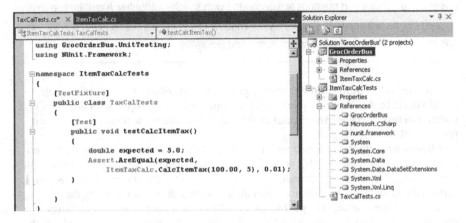

Figure 2-4. *Complete NUnit test method*

The NUnit GUI console, nunit.exe, can be launched from the start menu, by double-clicking the file in explorer, or however else you may be comfortable. When initially launched it will look like Figure 2-5.

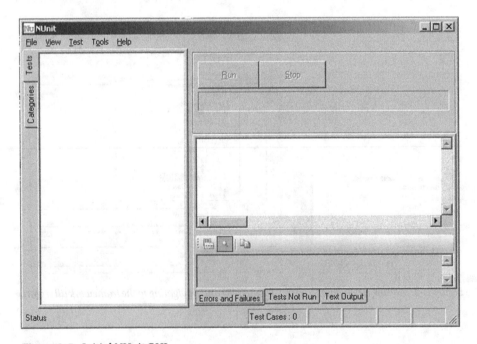

Figure 2-5. *Initial NUnit GUI*

From here we need to load our test assembly. To do this we click on the "File ➤ Open Project..." menu item and navigate to where our `ItemTaxCalcTests.dll` assembly is located. Once we open our assembly and can simply run the test. The output is shown in Figure 2-6; we have our original error back. To demonstrate that we can add additional tests without reloading our project, we will fix the error in the code and add an additional unit test as well.

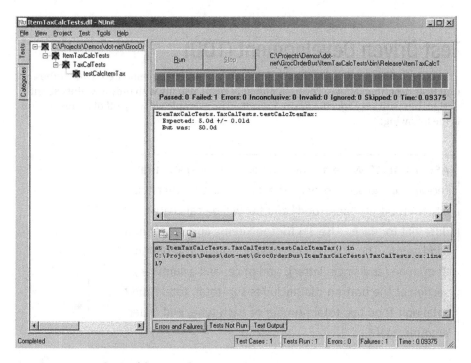

Figure 2-6. *Initial run of the tax calc test*

After we fix our calculation code, add the new test, and recompile the solution, our NUnit GUI will be updated once we switch back. Clicking "Run" or keying "F5" will give two successful tests, as shown in Figure 2-7.

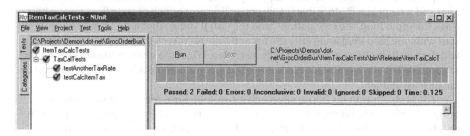

Figure 2-7. *Multiple passing test methods*

This gives us the same information as our JUnit tests performed earlier. Note that setup for NUnit was a little more involved; however the NUnit website (nunit.org) has some additional documentation on setting up NUnit as an external tool. This would allow its GUI to be launched from the menu bar and automatically load the test project. Also, as mentioned above premium versions of Visual Studio have a built in testing framework. The syntax is similar; more documentation is available via the Microsoft Visual Studio web site.

Test Driven Development (TDD)

Think about how programming assignments are typically implemented without the unit tests described above. The assignment is given, usually with only few hints about design, but with very specific desired results. The example we work off of in this section is the following:

ASSIGNMENT: Write a program that will generate a sales receipt for a grocery order. The items will be either typed as either "food" or "non-food" and tax will be calculated different for each. Use 3% for food items and 7% for non-food items. The final receipt should include a 3 column list – item, type (as a single letter), and price, and a summary section at the bottom that includes sub-total, total food tax, total non-food tax, total number of each type, and order amount total.

Figure 2-8. *Assignment for Unit Testing and TDD*

So what are you thinking? A command-line application with a while-loop for input? A keyword such as "total" to end the program? Or maybe a simple GUI with some input fields and two buttons for "Add Item" and "Total" with a scrollable text field for the receipt output? Regardless of the complexity of the user interface, how will you test the item and receipt logic? More than likely you will write a bunch of code first; for the Item class, the input loop, the calculations, and the GUI if you go that way. Then you would start with one food item and verify the tax and total is correct, then one non-food item, and then combinations, modifying code as you go. When the totals come out correct you are done! What you have produced is a working program and you're ready to move on to the next assignment.

The problem with the above approach is two-fold. First, other than running the program and examining the result there is no way to reliably test your program. This can be labor intensive, both for the developer and the professor checking out the program.

Writing unit tests as described above can help, but if they are done after-the-fact they might have limited validity; developers may have a tendency to write the test so the code passes, not writing the code so that it passes the test.

Also, what happens if the requirements change and/or get expanded? In a production software scenario change is inevitable. Users request new features; different versions of support systems are used; database support changes; etc. How can changes to a system be verified to not change the current functionality? One way is to have a system that is automatically testable so that any changes made can be verified to not introduce errors in existing code.

This brings us to Test Driven Development, TDD for short. TDD falls under the umbrella of agile software development, specifically at the component development level. The main tenet is to use unit tests as a method for driving the design of a component in an iterative process. The end result of the process is a completely functional component and a set of unit tests to verify that functionality. These same unit tests can be used when further modifications are made to the component to ensure the new modifications do not change the current functionality.

So what does the process look like? In short the steps are fairly simple:

> Write a unit test that tests the functionality to satisfy a given requirement.

> Run the test – it won't even compile because there is no supporting code yet.

> Write just enough code to successfully compile the test.

> Run the test – it will fail because no functionality has been put in the code.

> Write just enough code to satisfy the test.

> Run the test – it should now pass.

> Refactor the code as necessary, verifying with tests.

> Repeat until all requirements are coded and testable.

Because the application assignment is not presented in exactly a testable form, we are going to derive some specific, testable requirements from the original assignment. Some of these are a simple rephrasing of the above assignment goals. Others are assumptions made to clarify the unspecified operation of the system that we know must exist.

> Items are entered one at a time.

> Items are classified as "Food" or "non-food"; the default is "Food".

> The system determines whether the item is food or non-food.

> Food items are taxed at 3%, non-food at 7%.

> The system should keep a running total of item prices, including applicable tax.

Although we could probably derive a few more (we didn't even talk about determining item price), these will be enough to start the process of TDD. For brevity we won't complete the entire assignment; the reader is encouraged to take the result of this section and finish the assignment.

So we tackle our first requirement – items entered one at a time. We will use the .NET and NUnit tool, but the process would be the same with Eclipse and JUnit. After completing the setup outlined in the previous section we create our first unit test, shown in Listing 2-4.

Listing 2-4. First unit test for TDD

```
using NUnit.Framework;

namespace GrocOrderTests
{
    [TestFixture]
    public class OrderTests
    {
        [Test]
        public void testItemsEnteredOneAtATime()
        {
            CashRegister cr = new CashRegister();
            GrocItem gi_one = new GrocItem("Bread");
            cr.AddItem(gi_one);
            Assert.AreEqual(1, cr.ItemCount);
            GrocItem gi_two = new GrocItem("Milk");
            cr.AddItem(gi_two);
            Assert.AreEqual(2, cr.ItemCount);
        }
    }
}
```

If we try to compile this right now it won't even compile because the classes we're testing don't even exist yet. However, looking at the test we've already made some important assumptions:

GrocItem is our grocery item class

The GrocItem class has a constructor that takes a string parameter

We have a CashRegister class that acts as a container for GrocItems

CashRegister has and AddItem function for adding items.

CashRegister has an ItemCount method for tracking the number of items.

So now we'll write just enough of the above classes to make our solution compile successfully. The constructors will be empty. The ItemCount method will return 0; instead of a real value. Once we write enough code to allow the solution to compile, run the test in NUnit. It should fail, because even though our code compiles it is still a long way from complete. Listing 2-5 shows the initial code in the GrocOrder project.

Listing 2-5. Just enough code to compile

```
public class CashRegister
{

    public CashRegister()
    {
    }

    public void AddItem(GrocItem gi)
    {
    }

    public int ItemCount
    {
        get { return 0; }
    }

}

public class GrocItem
{
    public GrocItem(string Item)
    {
    }

}
```

Our next step is to go ahead and write enough code to make the test succeed. This is really pretty simple – just implement some fields to hold only the information we are currently testing and no more.

Listing 2-6. Just enough code to pass the test

```
public class CashRegister
{
    private List<GrocItem> _itemList
            = new List<GrocItem>();

    public CashRegister() {}
```

```
public void AddItem(GrocItem gi)
{
    _itemList.Add(gi);
}

public int ItemCount
{
    get { return
        _itemList.Count; }
}
}

public class GrocItem
{
    public String ItemName
    { get; set; }

    public GrocItem(string Item)
    {
        this.ItemName = ItemName;
    }

}
```

And that's it – our first test is coded to passing. At this point we can move on to our next requirement dealing with food type. So we make a new test, shown below.

Listing 2-7. Test for food type

```
[Test]
public void testDefaultFoodType()
{
    GrocItem gi = new GrocItem("Burger");

    Assert.AreEqual(FoodType.FOOD, gi.ItemFoodType);
}
```

As with the first test, a very simple concept but our test has led us to a couple of design decisions: an enumeration of "FoodType" and a property on the GrocItem class. Once we implement these simple concepts as shown in Listing 2-8, our test passes. Even though the concept and the implementation were both very simple, our solution is coming along.

Listing 2-8. Default FoodType of FOOD

```
namespace GrocOrder
{
    public enum FoodType
    {
        FOOD, NONFOOD
    }
```

```
public class GrocItem
{
    public String ItemName { get; set; }
    public FoodType ItemFoodType { get; set; }

    public GrocItem(string ItemName)
    {
        this.ItemName = ItemName;
        this.ItemFoodType = FoodType.FOOD;
    }

}
}
```

One of the benefits of this approach is that we are implementing only what is needed to pass the test. This should prevent our system from becoming too bloated with extra features and code that is rarely used. We don't have to worry too much about that with this assignment, but the principal also applies as the problems grow and become larger.

The next requirement is that the system determines the type of food. This wasn't exactly in the original problem statement but was derived from knowledge of how standard check-out systems work. True, we could let the user input the type of food with the product, but this isn't very practical nor does it simulate an actual order system very well. But it does beg the question – who defines the rules? In the case of the problem above, we do. This introduces us to another tenet of TDD – always start with the simplest solution first.

A statement such as "The system determines food or non-food" may elicit thoughts of a database lookup, a web-service call, or a collection-based cache of memory objects loaded into the system and referenced for every item. Those are all viable solutions and in a full-fledged system one of those would probably serve as the final implementation. However for our small problem statement we will define a much simpler system: a hard-coded comparison. The beauty of this approach is we have a test already defined, so whether or not we use a simple hard-coded lookup or a complex in-memory cache we can look up and ensure our system remains functional if the test passes. So let's write our test:

Listing 2-9. Determine food type test

```
[Test]
public void testFoodItemTypes()
{
    FoodTypeService fts = new FoodTypeService();

    GrocItem giFood = new GrocItem("Burger", fts);
    GrocItem giNonFood = new GrocItem("Light Bulb", fts);

    Assert.AreEqual(FoodType.FOOD, giFood.ItemFoodType);
    Assert.AreEqual(FoodType.NONFOOD, giNonFood.ItemFoodType);

}
```

Of course this doesn't compile because the FoodTypeService class doesn't exist and GrocItem doesn't have a constructor that takes two arguments. So we follow the same principle of coding just enough to let our test compile. As soon as we compile our code the NUnit project is updated to look like Figure 2-9, and once we press "Run" we have two tests that passed and our new test predictably fails, as shown in Figure 2-10. Again, since our project is very simple it may seem pointless to run all the tests just to see that the new test fails. However this is an important step – it assures us that nothing has changed as we added new classes to the system. Running the tests is quick and automated, and as we go forward, testing frequently after small code changes, isolating any potential fail becomes much easier.

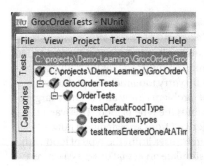

Figure 2-9. *NUnit test after compilation of new test*

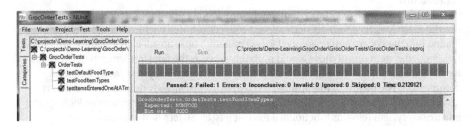

Figure 2-10. *Failed run of the new test*

Note that we also haven't done any refactoring yet – once the test passed the first time around we let it go at that and moved on. We will discuss refactoring in the next section.

To pass this test we simply finish creating our new functionality by implementing our stubbed out methods. The fully implemented classes are shown in Listing 2-10. Notice that since we are using a class to determine our food type with a switch statement. We could change this implementation at a later time to use a database or cached lookups. However since our test is in place, we could do this with confidence that we would not impact the system with our changes if all the tests continually passed.

Listing 2-10. Completed code for food item type

```
namespace GrocOrder
{
    public enum FoodType { FOOD, NONFOOD }

    public class GrocItem
    {
        public String ItemName { get; set; }
        public FoodType ItemFoodType { get; set; }

        public GrocItem(string ItemName)
        {
            this.ItemName = ItemName;
            this.ItemFoodType = FoodType.FOOD;
        }

        public GrocItem(string ItemName, FoodTypeService fts)
        {
            this.ItemName = ItemName;
            this.ItemFoodType = fts.DetermineFoodType(this.ItemName);
        }
    }
}
namespace GrocOrder
{
    public class FoodTypeService
    {
        public FoodType DetermineFoodType(string foodName)
        {
            FoodType ft = FoodType.FOOD;
            switch (foodName.ToUpper())
            {
                case "BURGER":
                case "BREAD":
                case "MILK":
                case "CEREAL":
                    ft = FoodType.FOOD;
                    break;
```

```
                case "LIGHT BULB":
                case "TOOTH PICKS":
                case "PAPER TOWELS":
                    ft = FoodType.NONFOOD;
                    break;
        }
        return ft;
    }
  }
}
```

The other two requirements; tax calculation and running total, are left for the reader. Simply apply the principles examined so far – write a test, make it compile, and then make it pass. Notice that before tax calculation can happen, you first have to determine the method for assigning an item price. But since there are tests already in place for type you can be sure that pricing won't have any effect on type.

Unit Testing Summary

Unit testing is a very important skill for writing software. It allows for automated verification of software functionality which is paramount to making changes with confidence. TDD allows for testing and designing "in-flight" which can not only help the speed at which code is developed, but provide a suite of tests for testing "in-flight" as well. We will discuss the values, benefits, and practices of TDD and unit testing going forward in the sections on refactoring and software methodologies.

CHAPTER 3

■ ■ ■

Refactoring

The single most important reference on software refactoring is the book *"Refactoring: Improving the Design of Existing Code"* by Martin Fowler, et al (1999). There have been many excellent publications since then but Fowler's book was one of the first to define the entire process and is the most often referenced. We cannot replicate the entire work here, nor should we attempt to take anything away from it; we will simply start with some realistic code in need of some help, demonstrate the power of refactoring, discuss the merits of the process, and demonstrate how modern tools can help.

Theory

First of all, what is refactoring? To many, refactoring is a fancy way of describing the process of "cleaning up" their code. But the scope is bigger than that. Yes, the code gets "cleaned up", but that is mostly as a result of refactoring, not its chief aim. Refactoring's overall purpose is to change the inner workings of existing code to reduce duplication, make the code easier to maintain, easier to modify in the future, and easier to understand, all without changing the functionality available to whomever is calling the code.

The strength in refactoring is that there are several standard techniques, identified and cataloged in *Refactoring* (1999). Refactorings listed in this reference will be denoted in bold for the rest of this section. Once these are learned they become easier to identify in code, implement, and discuss with fellow programmers. During a code review for instance, it may be that someone suggests you refactor the code using "extract method" and "replace switches with polymorphism." Knowing what these terms mean and how to apply them is what refactoring is all about.

So how do we make these changes without affecting the outside world? If the code being refactored was written via Test Driven Design (TDD) then there are already a set of unit tests to verify functionality. This was briefly mentioned in the section on TDD; refactoring can be a part of TDD as the code becomes more complicated. Even after all of the tests are written and pass it may be beneficial to go back and refactor sections of code.

If the original code was not written this way, then tests will need to be written to verify current functionality. Then these tests can be used throughout the refactoring to ensure the external functionality remains consistent.

Either way, having a set of tests to verify the external functionality of the code being refactored is very important. Again, the goal is to change the internals of the code only. By running the tests after each piece of refactoring the developer can have confidence that nothing was broken as a result of each refactoring change.

Software Demonstration Setup

Let us demonstrate refactoring by taking a look at some code that works as is and see how it might be refactored to become better code. In the example in Listing 3-2, we have completed a piece of code to handle the final operation of our TDD assignment given in Chapter 2. This is the code that will handle the total operation and the formatting of the receipt. Also, since we started with a unit test to verify the functionality, it is shown first in Listing 3-1 and shown that all tests pass in Figure 3-1.

Listing 3-1. Unit test for printFinalTotals()

```
@Test
public void testFinalSummaryOutput()
{
    PriceService ps = new PriceService();
    CashRegister cr = new CashRegister(ps);
    FoodTypeService fts = new FoodTypeService();

    String desiredOut = "Food Items: 2 NonFood Items: 1 Food Tax: 0.24
NonFood Tax: 0.14 Subtotal: 9.98 Order Total: 10.36";

    GrocItem giFood1 = new GrocItem("Burger", fts);
    GrocItem giFood2 = new GrocItem("Bread", fts);
    GrocItem giNonFood = new GrocItem("Light Bulb", fts);
    cr.AddItem(giFood1);
    cr.AddItem(giFood2);
    cr.AddItem(giNonFood);
    String receipt = cr.printFinalTotals();

    assertEquals(desiredOut, receipt);
}
```

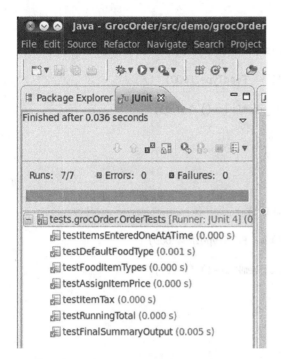

Figure 3-1. *All Tests passing*

Listing 3-2. printFinalTotal() method

```java
public String printFinalTotals()
{
    double tax1 = 0.0;
    double tax2 = 0.0;

    double total1 = 0.0;
    double total2 = 0.0;

    int numFood = 0;
    int numNonFood = 0;

    String output = null;
```

```java
// find food tax total
double runningTotal = 0.0;
for(GrocItem g : this._itemList)
{
    if ( g.get_itemFoodType() == FoodType.FOOD)
    {
        runningTotal += g.get_itemPrice() * 0.03;
    }
}
tax1 = runningTotal;

// find non-food tax total
runningTotal = 0.0;
for( GrocItem g : this._itemList)
{
    if ( g.get_itemFoodType() == FoodType.NONFOOD)
    {
        runningTotal += g.get_itemPrice() * 0.07;
    }
}
tax2 = runningTotal;

// Find sub total
runningTotal = 0.0;
for( GrocItem g : this._itemList)
{
    runningTotal += g.get_itemPrice();
}
total1 = runningTotal;

// Find number of each item
for( GrocItem g : this._itemList)
{
    if ( g.get_itemFoodType() == FoodType.FOOD)
    {
        numFood += 1;
    }
else
    {
        numNonFood += 1;
    }
}

// Find the total
total2 = total1 + tax1 + tax2;
```

```
    // piece together the string
    DecimalFormat df = new DecimalFormat("#.##");
    String numTotals = "Food Items: " + numFood + " NonFood Items: " +
numNonFood;
    String taxTotals = "Food Tax: " + df.format(tax1) + " NonFood Tax: " +
df.format(tax2);
    String totals = "Subtotal: " + df.format(total1) + " Order Total: " +
df.format(total2);

    output = numTotals + " " + taxTotals + " " + totals;

    // return the string
    return output;
}
```

So what do you see when looking at the above method? It works. It passed the test. So we should be done, right? Not quite. By looking at the code you should be able to see a few things that could be improved through refactoring:

> Some of the variable names are not very clear.

> The method itself is long and does several different things (i.e. a print method calculating tax).

> There are some magic number hard-coded values.

> Some of the code looks repetitive

> Repetitive use of a temporary variable

> Repeated concatenation of strings

Again, for a programming assignment this function will work. And none if the above listed issues seem like they would cause a great deal of grief. But if this routine was part of a program that had to be maintained, upgraded, and expanded over several years, these issues could very well cost a lot of time. Imagine coming back to this routine after 6 months on another project. What is tax1? What is total1? Why are there three different loops and what does each one do? These are the things that refactoring hopes to make clearer, both for ease of understanding and ease of modification.

A note About Tools

From the above snippet it can be seen that in this example we are using Java and Eclipse. Also, in Figure 3-1 it can be seen on the menu bar that there is a "Refactor" menu button. Many current software development tools, including Eclipse and Microsoft Visual Studio, have built-in support for many common refactorings. Use of these tools can both speed up the refactoring process and result in fewer errors as they reduce the amount of manual cut-and-paste and/or re-typing involved. We will mention the tools we are making use of as we go through our process. Keep in mind that other tools may not support the same refactorings as supported here, or may introduce new ones. Also, even after making use of an automated refactoring it may need to be manually touched up.

Refactoring the Code

Before we start with the refactoring let's recall the process of Test Driven Development; run the tests, change some code, run the tests again. The point is to keep the development changes short and run the tests often. If a running of the tests fails, the broken code has to be confined to the code we've changed since the last test. Often as we refactor, silly mistakes can creep in. These are things like not calling the new function, referring to the old instance of a variable when the name changes, not providing a concrete argument when a default is defined, etc. can really cause havoc. Using the automated tools mentioned above and keeping the test- development-support-test cycle short can help reduce the pain.

To follow our list above we will first address the problem with variable names. This is usually a simple to correct; the problems usually arise in missing an instance of the variable buried deep in a loop or within a large block of code. This is where the refactoring tool provided by the IDE is extremely useful.

Shown in Figure 3-2 is an example of the refactoring support offered in Eclipse, accessed by placing the cursor on the tax1 variable and pressing shift-alt-t. Note that refactoring is context-sensitive, so depending on what is highlighted and/or selected we may see a slightly different menu. In this case, we select Rename... and are presented with the instruction shown in Figure 3-3.

```
public String printFinalTotals()
{
    double tax1 = 0.0;
    double        Rename...                            Shift+Alt+R

    double        Move...                              Shift+Alt+V
    double
                  Change Method Signature...           Shift+Alt+C
    int num       Extract Local Variable...            Shift+Alt+L
    int num
                  Extract Constant...

    String        Inline...                            Shift+Alt+I

    // find       Convert Local Variable to Field...
    double
    for(Gro       Extract Interface...
    {
        if        Extract Superclass...
        {
                  Use Supertype Where Possible...

        }         Pull Up...
    }
    tax1 =        Push Down...

    // find       Extract Class...
    running
    for( Gr       Introduce Parameter Object...
    {
        if        Introduce Parameter...
        {
                  Generalize Declared Type...

                  Infer Generic Type Arguments...
```

Figure 3-2. *Refactoring support in IDE*

```
double  tax1  = 0.0;
double  tax2 = 0.0;
        Enter new name, press Enter to refactor  ▾
double
```

Figure 3-3. *Renaming instruction*

Once we enter our new name, `taxFood`, we can inspect the code and see that it has been updated in all the proper locations. Some IDEs may give the option for a preview for each instance to be renamed but in this case we don't use that. We then run the unit tests to make sure nothing is broken. While it is true we are using an automated refactoring tool there is still a chance something unexpected could break. Plus, the tests take less than a second, so why not be sure? We do this for each of the poorly named variables at the top of our method and replace each with a more descriptive name:

Original Name	Refactored Name
tax1	taxFood
tax2	taxNonFood
total1	subTotal
total2	orderTotal

After this we move to our next perceived issue – too long of a method. We solve this by using one of the most-used refactorings - **Extract Method**. This refactoring allows us to reduce the original method length by reducing repetitive code and pulling out distinct functionality into its own method that could be called by external code if needed.

Notice in our original code in Listing 3-2 that the method for calculating `tax1` (`taxFood`) and `tax2` (`taxNonFood`) are very similar. If we highlight our method and press the refactoring shortcut (`shift-alt-t`) we get the context menu shown in Figure 3-4, from which we choose `Extract Method...` to pull out the method.

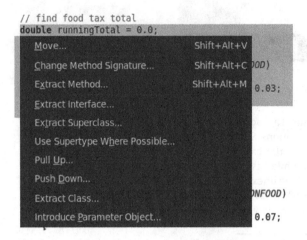

```
// find food tax total
double runningTotal = 0.0;
    Move...                          Shift+Alt+V
    Change Method Signature...       Shift+Alt+C  OD)
    Extract Method...                Shift+Alt+M  0.03;
    Extract Interface...
    Extract Superclass...
    Use Supertype Where Possible...
    Pull Up...
    Push Down...
    Extract Class...                          NFOOD)
    Introduce Parameter Object...             0.07;
```

Figure 3-4. Refactoring menu for multiple lines

This is a little more involved than simple renaming, and selecting the menu item brings up a dialog where we have some options. This dialog is shown in Figure 3-5. Completing the dialog will create the extracted method for us and the tool replaces our code with a function call. We run our tests and they all pass, but we're still not quite satisfied with the code.

Extract Method

Method name: calculateTaxTotal

Access modifier: ○ public ○ protected ○ default ● private

☐ Declare thrown runtime exceptions
☐ Generate method comment
☐ Replace additional occurrences of statements with method

Method signature preview:
private double calculateTaxTotal()

Preview >   Cancel   OK

Figure 3-5. Extract Method dialog

While we could move on with some other refactorings, we will clean up this method call and then the method.

Listing 3-3. Replaced code and extracted method

```
// replaced code inside of original method
double runningTotal = calculateTaxTotal();
taxFood = runningTotal;

// newly extracted method
private double calculateTaxTotal()
{
    double runningTotal = 0.0;
    for(GrocItem g : this._itemList)
    {
        if ( g.get_itemFoodType() == FoodType.FOOD)
            runningTotal += g.get_itemPrice() * 0.03;
    }
    return runningTotal;
}
```

The first thing to do is to reduce the statement from two lines to one. There is no need for the runningTotal variable in this expression; the function result can be assigned directly to taxFood. In the refactoring catalog this is called **Inline Temp**.

To complete our refactoring and eliminate duplicate code, we need to modify the method signature. By looking at the original code, the only difference between the two loops was the tax rate which was determined by food type. If we passed these in as parameters the method would be generic enough to use anywhere. So let's change our method signature, which is also a menu item in Figure 3-4. Clicking this will bring us the dialog for changing the method signature. In Figure 3-6 I've already added the new parameters for the method.

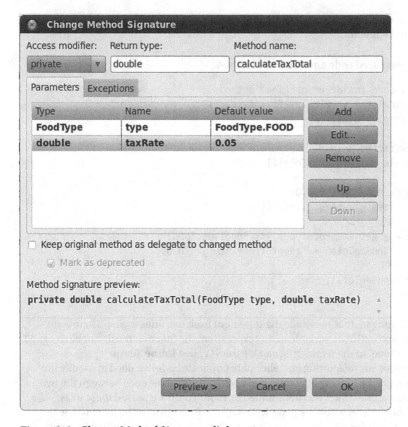

Figure 3-6. *Change Method Signature dialog*

The Preview button will show you how the new signature will look as well as give you warnings if there are issues with the parameters. Clicking "OK" or "Preview >" and then "Finish" will change the signature of the targeted method. Save and run the test. It passes because we haven't changed the method to use the parameters. After we change the method to use the parameters we save and run the tests. Oops! The test fails! What did we do?

Turns out the default value we included in the function signature dialog was not the same as the value we were currently using is code. This was done on purpose, as forgetting to adjust the function input value will lead to a failing test. After typing in the correct value we re-run the tests again and now it passes. In a real system we might want to add an additional test for this new function; one to test the default parameters and one for passed-in values, but we won't do that in this short example.

After we make the adjustments to the non-food loop we have some code that is clearly better structured than what was there to start.

Listing 3-4. Extracted tax calculation with parameters

```
// replaced code inside of original method
taxFood = calculateTaxTotal(FoodType.FOOD, 0.03);

taxNonFood = calculateTaxTotal(FoodType.NONFOOD, 0.07);

// refactored method
private double calculateTaxTotal(FoodType type,
                                double taxRate)
{
    double runningTotal = 0.0;
    for(GrocItem g : this._itemList)
    {
        if ( g.get_itemFoodType() == type)
            runningTotal += g.get_itemPrice() * taxRate;
    }
    return runningTotal;
}
```

The final refactoring to apply to this code is to get rid of the "magic numbers" for the tax rates. In a real system we may dynamically get the rates at run-time or via a price service component. In our example we will apply the **Replace Magic Number with Symbolic Constant** refactoring to provide a level of abstraction. Notice in Figure 3-2 there is menu item for "Extract Constant". If we select our magic number, bring up the refactoring menu by pressing shift-alt-t and choose "Extract Constant", we will be shown the dialog in Figure 3-7. This dialog lets us give our desired constant a name along with some other specifications.

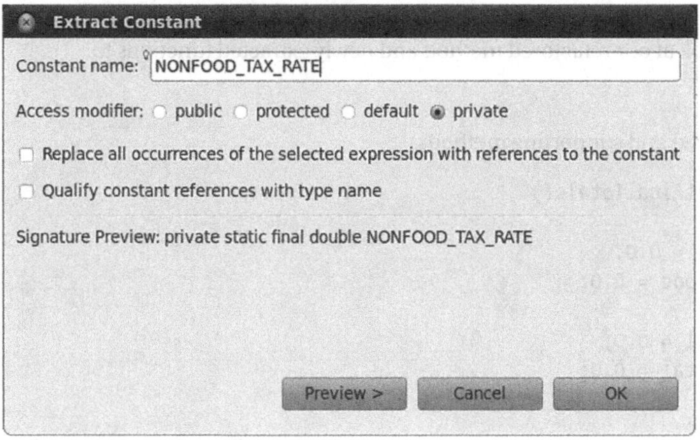

Figure 3-7. *Extract Constant options*

We perform this refactoring for both the food tax and non-food tax. These constants will be declared at the top of our class and will replace the hard-coded values in the calls to calculateTaxTotal. We again verify nothing is broken by running our unit tests after each change. So far so good.

We can use the same **Extract Method** refactoring for the sub-total entry as well. Following the same process as before, we highlight the sub-total loop and open the Refactoring context menu. We choose "Extract Method" and choose our method name as calculateOrderSubTotal.

The final loop for calculating the number of each type of item is a little trickier. If we simply highlight the loop and try to use "Extract Method" directly from the menu we get an error:

Inside of the loop, we assign to either one of the variable mentioned in Figure 3-8 based on the type of item. This means that we will have to handle this refactoring manually because we have to make some choices. Do we want to create a class with two fields and pass the object to the function? Or use an array? Or a function call that takes FoodType as a parameter and returns the count? Even though this last option will mean two calls to the function to assign the two different values, this is the approach we use.

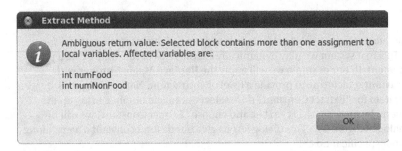

Figure 3-8. *Extract method error*

So let's take a look at our refactored method and newly extracted functions to support it:

Listing 3-5. Refactored and supporting methods

```
public String printFinalTotals()
{
    double taxFood = 0.0;
    double taxNonFood = 0.0;

    double subTotal = 0.0;
    double orderTotal = 0.0;

    int numFood = 0;
    int numNonFood = 0;

    String output = null;
```

```
        // find food tax total
        taxFood = calculateTaxTotal(FoodType.FOOD, FOOD_TAX_RATE);

        // find non-food tax total
        taxNonFood = calculateTaxTotal(FoodType.NONFOOD,
                                        NONFOOD_TAX_RATE);

        // Find sub total
        subTotal = calculateOrderSubTotal();

        // Find number of each item
        numFood = numItemsByType(FoodType.FOOD);
        numNonFood = numItemsByType(FoodType.NONFOOD);

        // Find the total
        orderTotal = subTotal + taxFood + taxNonFood;

        // piece together the string
        DecimalFormat df = new DecimalFormat("#.##");
        String numTotals = "Food Items: " + numFood +
                            "NonFood Items: " + numNonFood;
        String taxTotals = "Food Tax: " + df.format(taxFood) +
                            " NonFood Tax: " + df.format(taxNonFood);
        String totals = "Subtotal: " + df.format(subTotal) +
                        " Order Total: " + df.format(orderTotal);

        output = numTotals + " " + taxTotals + " " + totals;

        // return the string
        return output;
    }

    private int numItemsByType(FoodType ft)
    {
        int numItems = 0;
        for( GrocItem g : this._itemList)
        {
            if ( g.get_itemFoodType() == ft)
            {
                numItems += 1;
            }
        }
        return numItems;
    }
```

```
private double calculateOrderSubTotal()
{
    double runningTotal = 0.0;

    for( GrocItem g : this._itemList)
    {
        runningTotal += g.get_itemPrice();
    }
    return runningTotal;
}

private double calculateTaxTotal(FoodType type, double taxRate)
{
    double runningTotal = 0.0;
    for(GrocItem g : this._itemList)
    {
        if ( g.get_itemFoodType() == type)
        {
            runningTotal += g.get_itemPrice() * taxRate;
        }
    }
    return runningTotal;
}
```

So are we done? The refactored printFinalTotals() is certainly cleaner and more understandable than the original. We have some helper methods that each do a single calculation and have parameterized them were possible to eliminate duplicate code. And we've ensured that the end result is the same by verifying each change with our unit tests.

While our new method is certainly cleaner and clearer than before, there are two things that can be addressed. First, there is a refactoring called **Replace Temp with Query**. In our refactored method we have a lot of temporary storage holders that are used only once or twice in the entire method. Why not remove the temporary assignment and put the function call in its place? Second, we've extracted a method for tax and subtotal, but the print method is still calculating the order total. To properly structure the code the order total should be in its own method as well; the print method should only construct a print string. The fully refactored print method is shown in Figure 3-6. Extracting the calculateOrderTotal method and further refactoring the printFinalTotals method is left as an exercise for the reader.

Summary

In this section we demonstrated how to apply refactoring to a method to make it more concise and easier to understand. Through the combination with unit testing the outward facing functionality was kept consistent. We ended up with not only a print method that was more consistent, but also with several pieces of functionality that could be made available to other client code. This would reduce the redundancy and also make the code easer to modify.

We have only touched the surface with a few standard refactorings. Many other publications are available that expand on the early work in *Refactoring* (1999). The reader is encouraged to review the sites and books listed in the Bibliography and Additional Reading sections for further information.

In addition, refactoring using patterns will be discussed later in Chapter 7. That section will show how the combination of refactoring and design patterns can turn a basic prototype into a well-design scalable system. ( )

Listing 3-6. Fully Refactored print method

```java
public String printFinalTotals()
{
    String output = null;

    // piece together the string
    DecimalFormat df = new DecimalFormat("#.##");
    String numTotals = "Food Items: " + numItemsByType(FoodType.FOOD)
        + " NonFood Items: "
        + numItemsByType(FoodType.NONFOOD);

    String taxTotals = "Food Tax: "
        + df.format(calculateTaxTotal(FoodType.FOOD, FOOD_TAX_RATE))
        + " NonFood Tax: "
        + df.format(calculateTaxTotal(FoodType.NONFOOD,
                                      NONFOOD_TAX_RATE));

    String totals = "Subtotal: " + df.format(calculateOrderSubTotal())
        + " Order Total: " + df.format(calculateOrderTotal());

    output = numTotals + " " + taxTotals + " " + totals;

    // return the string
    return output;
}
```

■ ■ ■

CHAPTER 4

Build Tools and Continuous Integration

When compiling a stand-alone application as part of a programming assignment, or even with a team of other students for a senior project, compilation is usually done manually from within the Integrated Development Environment (IDE). Both Microsoft Visual Studio and Eclipse have menu options and shortcut keys for compiling an application. Often times if a piece of software has dependent components such as external assemblies or JAR files these are manually copied from a shared directory or some other library sharing mechanism.

When projects become larger, more complex, and the development team more dispersed, a different system is often used. An automated build system is usually employed, and this system may or may not include continuous integration (CI). In this section we first explain build tools, and then conclude with what CI is and how it works.

Make

The original build tool was the make utility; a command line tool for compiling an executable based on rules, dependencies, and commands. The GNU implementation of make is included on most Linux distributions and it is still very common for compiling C and C++ programs. Tools and utilities for Linux that have downloadable source usually include a makefile so that if desired the user can build the utility from the source.

A simple example will show the basics of make. First, let's assume we are in a Linux environment and have a very simple C++ program with 5 files – a helloworld.cpp with our main method, and two classes, Bob and Cindy, each with a .cpp and .h file for their definition and declaration. The main function simply creates an instance of the Bob and Cindy classes and calls their only method, SayHello(). How would we compile this? The command line would look like Listing 4-1.

Listing 4-1. Command for manual C++ compile

```
g++ -o hellobobandcindy helloworld.cpp cBob.cpp cCindy.cpp
```

While this would certainly work, especially in an environment such as the bash shell where the up-arrow could be used to repeat the previous command, it could get unwieldy very quickly as the number of files increased.

Using make to manage larger projects involves creating a makefile for the project. A makefile is simply a text file that follows some special formatting rules. The file lists the "targets" to be built and the dependencies for each target. This can save a tremendous amount of time when a project is hundreds of files and only a few need recompiled. A sample makefile is shown in Listing 4-2. To compile the user would simply type the command "make" on the command line. By default, the make utility looks for a file with the name of "makefile" in the current directory. Command-line options allow for the specification of other names but we won't document all the options here.

Listing 4-2. Sample make file

```
CC=g++
OBJDEPS = helloworld.o cBob.o cCindy.o

all: hellobobandcindy

hellobobandcindy: $(OBJDEPS)
        $(CC) -o hellobobandcindy $(OBJDEPS)
helloworld.o: helloworld.cpp
        $(CC) -c helloworld.cpp
cBob.o: cBob.cpp cBob.h
        $(CC) -c cBob.cpp
cCindy.o: cCindy.cpp cCindy.h
        $(CC) -c cCindy.cpp

clean:
        rm *.o hellobobandcindy
```

While this certainly looks more complex than the original "g++" command, the advantages are in repeatability, scalability, and target/rule based processing. First, typing make is much easier than remembering the entire compile command. Secondly, as we add files to the project we can simply follow the pattern already there, each source and header file creates an object file; the main executable is dependent on those source files. Makefiles with several dozen if not hundreds of source files are common in enterprise projects.

Finally, we can control our project through targets based on rules. In make, a rule consists of three parts; the target, the dependencies, and the command. Targets are on the left side of the colon (:), dependencies are on the right side, and the command to execute is on the line below preceded by a tab. So executing "make clean" on the command line would invoke the "clean" target and remove all the object files and our hellobobandcindy file. Notice we've also used some macro definitions (CC=g++) that we can replace later in the rules with the $() syntax.

We've only scratched the surface of the make tool but the above sample and discussion should allow for interpreting most makefiles, even if they are significantly more complex. However for additional information the reader should consult some resources listed in the "Suggested Reading" or "Bibliography" section.

Ant

Ant is the de facto standard for compiling in the Java environment. Like make it relies on targets, dependencies, and commands, but the syntax is completely different. Ant uses an XML document to describe a project and XML elements to list commands. A very simple ant file is shown in Listing 4-3. This file is named build.xml, would be placed in the project root directory, and would be invoked from the command line by simply typing "ant" in that directory.

Listing 4-3. Sample ANT build file

```
<?xml version="1.0"?>
<project name="HelloJavaAnt" default="build">
        <property name="src.dir"      location="src" />
        <property name="build.dir"    location="build/classes" />

        <target name="mkdir">
                <mkdir dir="${build.dir}" />
                <mkdir dir="${build.dir}/JARs" />
        </target>

        <target name="build" depends="mkdir">
                <javac srcdir="${src.dir}"
                        destdir="${build.dir}"/>
        </target>

        <target name="compress" depends="build">
                <jar destfile="${build.dir}/JARs"
                        basedir="${build.dir}"
        </target>

</project>
```

Some tools can use Ant behind the scenes and maintain the build.xml file as part of the project management. In this case the developer doesn't have to maintain the complex XML file. This allows for easy building through the tool and also for scripting of the build via command-line tools.

Even though this is a very simple build script it illustrates some very important concepts. There are properties defined and referenced, named targets, dependencies, and commands. Notice these are all either XML elements or attributes. In the script above the properties are defined at the top of the file but they could also have been defined in a separate file. The properties defined in the separate file would be brought in with an <import> task. This is common in larger projects and also in projects that use a build file to go through several environments such as a development environment, a testing environment, and finally to production. The core build file can remain the same in all environments and any environment-specific settings can be in the separate file that changes per environment.

Ant also has a task for running JUnit tests which will discuss more when we talk about Continuous Integration. It is important to note that there are many more tasks than mentioned here; the reader should consult the Ant online documentation (http://ant.apache.org/manual/) or one of the references listed in the back for a complete task list. It is also extensible, meaning that custom actions can be written if needed; however the list of pre-written commands is usually adequate for even the most complex of projects.

NAnt/MSBuild

NAnt is a .NET equivalent of the Ant tool; it is written to use Microsoft-centric tasks and actions and is open source. At the time of writing it is available on SourceForge (http://nant.sourceforge.net). An example NAnt script is shown in Listing 4-4.

Listing 4-4. Sample NAnt build file

```xml
<?xml version="1.0"?>
<project name="HelloNant" default="build" basedir=".">
        <description>Building HelloWorld in NANT</description>
        <property name="debug" value="true" overwrite="false" />

        <target name="clean" description="remove generated files">
                <delete file="HelloNant.exe" failonerror="false" />
                <delete file="HelloNant.pdb" failonerror="false" />
        </target>

        <target name="build" description="build hello world with Nant">
                <csc target="exe" output="HelloNant.exe"
                    debug="${debug}">
                        <sources>
                                <includes name="HelloNant.cs" />
                        </sources>
                </csc>
        </target>
</project>
```

Notice the similarities to the Ant script shown in the previous section. In fact, except for the <csc> command to execute the C-Sharp compiler instead of <javac> it would be hard to distinguish between the two. Like Ant, NAnt also has many more tasks than are shown here, including file manipulation tasks such as <copy>, <move>, and <mkdir> as well as an <nunit> task for running unit tests. The above file could be named anything but with a .build extension. Located in the project root directory it would simply be invoked from the command line by typing "NAnt".

MSBuild is Microsoft's core compilation tool for the .NET Framework. It also relies on an Ant-like XML build file, found as the project files (.vbproj or .csproj) in a typical .Net solution. While it is possible to write an MSBuild build file by hand, more commonly it is used behind the scenes by Visual Studio to compile the projects in a solution.

Build settings and configurations changed through the IDE are represented in the project files. When using MSBuild through the IDE the user may never have to know the details or structure of the build file. However the tool itself is a command-line utility and is available as part of the .NET Framework SDK.

Maven

Although generally thought of as an alternative to Ant, Maven is more than a build tool. In addition to building source code it is a set of conventions for the code repository structure and managing the project lifecycle. In fact one of the major tenets of Maven is "convention over configuration" (Sonatype, 2008).

Maven has a conventional definition for a project, known as the Project Object Model, or POM (Sonatype, 2008). It is assumed that directories exist in specific locations and a typical series of events (build, compress, deploy) are followed. For example, while Ant relies on explicit settings for directories, shown in Listing 4-3 as src.dir and build.dir, Maven expects by default for source code to be in the directory project_dir/src/main/java, where project_dir is the main project directory. Compiled classes will go into project_dir/target/classes directory and a JAR file will be created in project_dir/target. With these conventions in place the build file, named pom.xml and residing in the main project directory, can be as simple as the example in Listing 4-5. Running Maven to build the project is done by typing mvn install from the command line in the main project directory where pom.xml is located.

Listing 4-5. Very simple Maven pom.xml

```
<project>
        <modelVersion>4.0.0</modelVersion>
        <groupId>com.yourcompany.MavenProject</groupID>
        <artifactId>HelloMaven</artifactId>
        <version>2.0.0</version>
        <description>Simple Maven Project</description>
</project>
```

Note that this is a bare-bones POM file. A more typical POM could have additional sections for dependencies, packaging, exclusions, plugins, and more. The intent of the above example is that by following the conventions laid out by Maven, configuration can be minimal. The meaning of the above elements are as follows:

- modelVersion – the version of the POM model this file is referencing

- groupId – unique identifier for the organization creating the project

- artifactId – unique identifier of the result of this POM file, such as the name of the output JAR file, in this case HelloMaven.jar

- version – unique version of the produced artifact

- description – simple description of the project, often used for documentation

A more complete and practical example is shown in Listing 4-6. This snippet includes a few additional tags as well as a dependencies section. The <dependencies> section lists external libraries that the project needs in <dependency> elements. In this case, the project needs the log4j external library file (logging with log4j is discussed in Chapter 5) for logging purposes. Listing it in this manner instructs the mvn tool to include this file when it compiles the application. The fields groupId, artifactId, and version behave as for the parent project file but identify these items for the dependency and are used for lookup in the repository (more on that below). The scope setting is also required and identifies when the library is needed. The compile entry means the library is needed to compile and run the project.

Listing 4-6. Maven POM with dependency

```
<project>
        <modelVersion>4.0.0</modelVersion>
        <groupId>com.yourcompany.MavenProject</groupID>
        <artifactId>HelloMaven</artifactId>
        <packaging>jar</packaging>
        <name>Expanded Maven</name>
        <version>2.0.0</version>
        <dependencies>
          <dependency>
            <groupId>log4j</groupId>
            <artifactId>log4j</artifactId>
            <version>1.2.9</version>
            <scope>compile</scope>
          </dependency>
        </dependencies>
        <description>Simple Maven Project</description>
</project>
```

When Maven sees the dependency entry it will first check the local repository for the entry. The local repository is maintained by Maven to store artifacts that are frequently referenced. These files and resources are kept locally both for improved compilation speed and to reduce repetitive network overhead. However, if the desired resource is not found in the local repository, a remote repository is searched. By default the Maven central repository at http://repo.maven.apache.org/maven2/ is used, but mirrors can also be specified if desired. To find resources that are available from the Maven repository the website (at the time of this writing) is http://search.maven.org/#browse.

Organizations may also setup an internal repository that mimics the structure of the official maven repository. This would allow developers to reference an intranet-based repository and would limit external traffic. It would also allow internal libraries to be placed in the repository without publishing them for public consumption.

To demonstrate the process of expanding the POM file in Listing 4-6, two libraries will be added; one a (imaginary) custom library from an internal repository, the other the JUnit JAR from the central repository.

To find the groupId, artifactId, and version the repository should be consulted to find the information. Browsing to the URL given above, the information for obtaining the latest JUnit JAR is "junit", "junit", and "4.10", respectively, and it will only be used for our test cases.

The internal repository should be set up in the same way and allow us to browse for library components. For the example the customLibrary.jar file, version 1.6, will be referenced. This file will be part of the application and should be available at run time, similar to the log4j library.

Note that in the dependency elements, the repository for the component is not specified. The Maven application will search both the default repositories and any specified in the POM file until it finds the specified resource. If the resource is needed at compile-time and cannot be found the build will fail.

Listing 4-7. POM file with internal repository and multiple dependencies

```
<project>
        <modelVersion>4.0.0</modelVersion>
        <groupId>com.yourcompany.MavenProject</groupID>
        <artifactId>HelloMaven</artifactId>
        <packaging>jar</packaging>
        <name>Expanded Maven</name>
        <version>2.0.0</version>
        <repositories>
          <id>internal-repository</id>
          <name>Internal Corporate Repository</name>
          <url>http://internal.url.here/repo</url>
        </repositories>
        <dependencies>
          <dependency>
              <groupId>log4j</groupId>
              <artifactId>log4j</artifactId>
              <version>1.2.9</version>
              <scope>compile</scope>
          </dependency>
          <dependency>
              <groupId>junit</groupId>
              <artifactId>junit</artifactId>
              <version>4.10</version>
              <scope>test</scope>
          </dependency>
          <dependency>
              <groupId>com.company-url</groupId>
              <artifactId>customLibrary</artifactId>
              <version>1.6.0</version>
              <scope>compile</scope>
          </dependency>
        </dependencies>
        <description>Simple Maven Project</description>
</project>
```

Continuous Integration (CI) Tools

As we've said, many developers, even when part of a larger team, will usually compile software through an IDE. Tools that use Ant files for building often automate the process with a "Build..." menu command, as do Visual Studio for .Net (using MSBuild) and C++ tools such as Code Blocks (using GCC or other C++ compilers). So when are file-based command-line build scripts used? By far the most common use of build scripts is for continuous integration, also known as CI. A developer may not interact with these systems directly but knowledge of them is sometimes necessary for release planning.

CI is predominately used in environments which require repository code to always successfully compile. Schedules may vary depending on several factors such as number of developers, time-zone/location (domestic vs. off-shore), stage of development, or other corporate, department, or team standards. Although the ultimate goal of CI is to respond to every source code check-in by running and verifying a build, other schedules are common such as hourly builds, nightly builds and weekly builds. As with TDD the shorter the cycle the easier it is to find the code that causes a build to fail.

CI products are typically servers or have service or daemon components which continually run. They typically work in conjunction with source code repositories (described in Chapter 1: Version Control) and can continually monitor the repository for new code. CI servers are usually integrated with some type of web dashboard and/or an email alerting system. At any time a user can view the dashboard to see the results of the latest build, review build artifacts, historical build times, and other information depending on the particular product. Automated email notifications can be configured to go to members of the team letting them know new code is available in the repository in the event of a successful build. An email alert is also typical to let the team know when bad code has been checked in and the build failed. This type of continuous feedback can ensure that code remains in a valid state in the repository. Anytime code is checked in that causes a failure the team is notified quickly and can take steps to resolve the issue before a lot of damage is done.

A CI system's ability to do unit tests as part of the build process is also very beneficial to the state of the code in the repository. If the unit tests are run as soon as the code is built it can alert users to failed tests immediately after check-in. This also helps reduce bugs in the long term because this extra step of automated unit testing helps to catch logic errors that may pass the compile step but break a logic condition in the system.

Simple Example

As mentioned above, Continuous Integration is mostly accomplished by server products. Some common products include AnthillPro, CruiseControl, and Microsoft Team Foundation Server, and many others. For a local "proof of concept" a simple batch file-based CI tool will be shown, taken from a similar discussion in (Arkin &Millet, 2009).

Recall that there are several ways to manually compile both .NET and Java applications. The compilers themselves can be called from the command-line (cs or javac), or a build tool (msbuild, ant, nant or mvn) can be ran with a suitable configuration file. Additionally, recall that underneath the TortoiseSVN shell is the svn.exe executable that can be used to communicate with the SVN repository. Given those facts then it is possible to use a script to do the following:

1. Periodically check the repository for source file changes.

2. If changes are found, pull the source from the repository.

3. Build the code and copy it to a release location.

4. If desired, email the development team with the results of the build.

To complete this very simple example of how a CI server could be emulated locally, a batch file is created. It will handle the first three steps outlined above with the intent of keeping a local working directly in sync with the repository. The placement of the file is unimportant but the paths, whether relative or absolute, must be correct. In the case of the file shown in Listing 4-8, the file is located in c:\Projects and the project being checked is located in c:\Projects\Console\ConsoleBranch.

Listing 4-8. Batch file for emulating a CI server

```
@ECHO OFF
SET mod_string=""

FOR /F "tokens=*" %%A IN ('svn update Console\ConsoleBranch') DO SET
mod_string=%%A
SET firstchar=%mod_string:~0,1%
IF %firstchar%==U goto autocompile
echo "no changes"
exit
:autocompile
echo "changes detected - auto compiling"
msbuild Console\ConsoleBranch.sln
copy Console\bin\Release\*.* \\deploy\Console
exit
```

While understanding the batch syntax is not necessary, a few actions can be pointed out to highlight the steps:

1. The command-line call "svn update Console\ConsoleBranch" produces an output that is stored in a variable "mod_string"

2. The first character of the "mod_string" variable is extracted

3. If the first character is "U" (which stands for Update) then at least one file was updated by svn, meaning a newer copy was pulled from the repository and successfully merged with the local working copy. Control is "jumped" to the "autocompile" label and the msbuild compiler is used to recompile the local code.

4. The compiled code and all contents of the Release folder are copied to an external deployment location, in this case a network shared folder.

5. If no update was found the batch prints a message and exits.

This batch file could be called in several ways. It could be executed manually by the developer every day before coding. An automated task could be set up within the Windows Scheduler to execute at a certain time or times every day.

Also, this batch is not very robust. It is only meant to work on a single developer's workstation and check only for file updates from the repository. Other events such as files being added ("A") or deleted ("D") in the repository would be missed by this batch. In addition there could be a conflict produced by the update; this is also not handled by this simple batch.

Deploying to Environments

Once a software component has been successfully built, the next step is to deploy or distribute it. Whereas retail software is normally distributed and installed via disc or download, enterprise and internal components are generally deployed directly to servers. Deeper discussions of multiple environments and architecture are given in Appendix A and Chapter 7, but in general the developer will not have access rights to any servers other than development. This necessitates that deployment to testing and production servers be handled by other teams; a common way is to automate the process through the CI system.

While the actual deployments to multiple environments are handled by the CI software, the developer must take care to make sure the application still functions correctly in each environment. How is that done? And what does it have to do with deployments? This section answers that question and discusses some common techniques that developers can use to solve this problem.

The answer is that although there are various methods to accomplish this, a very common one is to abstract environment-specific settings out into an external properties file. This may include database connection strings, file paths, error messages, or even some text labels. In Java environments this is typically a .properties file that typically uses a name=value syntax. In the .NET world the configuration file is a .config file that uses an XML-based property mechanism. An example of a Java property file and how to read it is shown in Listing 4-9 and Listing 4-10 on the next page. Keep in mind in a real application these settings would be used while constructing file paths, database connection strings, or other critical dynamic information, not simply read and then printed back out.

Listing 4-9. Sample Java property file (settings.properties)

```
db.server=servername
db.dbname=databasename
file.upload=upload_folder_name
file.temp=temp_folder_name
```

Listing 4-10. Reading a properties file in Java

```
public static void main(String[] args)
{
    Properties prop = new Properties();

    prop.load(new FileInputStream("settings.properties"));

    // get each property value and print it out
    System.out.println(prop.getProperty("db.server"));
    System.out.println(prop.getProperty("db.dbname"));
    System.out.println(prop.getProperty("file.upload"));
    System.out.println(prop.getProperty("file.temp"));
}
```

The .NET version is similar, shown in Listing 4-11 and Listing 4-12. In .NET the file isn't manually read as the configuration filename follows a convention based on the executable. This is not unique to .NET however. Naming conventions such as this are often applied in configuration and other frameworks in both .NET and Java to standardize a base location for settings, either used by the framework in question or user-defined values. Some configuration frameworks even allow for automatic setting-to-object-property mapping, meaning that the settings would be automatically loaded and referenced similar to Propclass.db_server, but that is beyond the scope of this discussion.

Listing 4-11. Sample .NET configuration file (ConsoleBranch.exe.config)

```
<configuration>
    <appSettings>
        <add key="db.server" value="servername"/>
        <add key="db.dbname" value="databasename"/>
        <add key="file.upload" value="upload_folder_name"/>
        <add key="file.temp" value="temp_folder_name"/>
    </appSettings>
</configuration>
```

Listing 4-12. Reading properties in .NET

```
class Program
{
    static void Main(string[] args)
    {
        Console.WriteLine(ConfigurationManager.
                            AppSettings.Get("db.server"));
        Console.WriteLine(ConfigurationManager.
                            AppSettings.Get("db.dbname"));
        Console.WriteLine(ConfigurationManager.
                            AppSettings.Get("file.upload"));
        Console.WriteLine(ConfigurationManager.
                            AppSettings.Get("file.temp"));
    }
}
```

Once these settings have been externalized there are several ways to adjust them to become environment-aware. In some instances there may be a single configuration file with all the environment settings differentiated by a naming convention. This would be done by duplicating the lines in the file but adding an identifier to each one, such as db.test.server, db.prod.server, etc. In this method the application itself is aware of its environment and chooses the appropriate settings based on that knowledge. This technique has the advantage of deploying a single file into each environment, as well as only maintaining a single file. While this certainly works, the file can become cluttered and confusing with all settings for all environments in one file. In addition, making the application aware of the environment is often not the best choice.

A better way that leverages the power of the CI deployment tools is to have multiple files, one per environment. The files will have the same setting names in each, but each will have the correct environment specific value. This results in more files, but each one is specific to one environment. A CI tool used for deployment will generally have multiple deployment workflows or scripts, also one per environment. Each workflow can deploy the actual software component that was built previously in the CI step (jar, exe, dll, etc.) along with the correct environment-specific settings file. A step at the end of the deployment would rename the copied settings file to the file name the component expects: "rename settings.test.properties settings.properties".

Listing 4-13. Batch file for testing deployment

```
@ECHO OFF
echo "TESTING DEPLOY"
copy \\deploy\Console\*.exe \\test_server\programs\console
copy \\deploy\Console\*.dll \\test_server\programs\console
copy \\deploy\Console\Console.TEST.config \\test_server\programs\console
rename \\test_server\programs\console\Console.TEST.config
        \\test_server\programs\console\Console.exe.config
echo "TESTING DEPLOY COMPLETE"
exit
```

Listing 4-13 and Listing 4-14 show examples that expand on the CI batch file of Listing 4-8. Recall from that script the output was copied to a deployment folder; these batch files copy the correct artifacts from that folder to the appropriate runtime location and perform the appropriate name manipulation. These files are obviously over-simplifications of what an actual CI deployment would do but the concept is the same.

Listing 4-14. Batch file for production deploy

```
@ECHO OFF
echo "PRODUCTION DEPLOY"
copy \\deploy\Console\*.exe \\prod_server\programs\console
copy \\deploy\Console\*.dll \\prod_server\programs\console
copy \\deploy\Console\Console.PROD.config \\prod_server\programs\console
rename \\test_server\programs\console\Console.PROD.config
       \\test_server\programs\console\Console.exe.config
echo "PRODUCTION DEPLOY COMPLETE"
exit
```

Summary

Single user builds are usually done through an IDE, even when part of a larger project. These IDE builds may actually make use of a script- or xml-based utility but the user rarely needs to know. However when this process moves to an automated system of build, test, and deploy the benefits of continuous integration become apparent. In addition, when deploying to multiple environments it is useful to be able to use a configuration framework and the CI system to support a single build through the environments. The scripts demonstrated in this chapter, though simple, should give the reader the basics to use and expand command-line based build tools if needed.

CHAPTER 5

■ ■ ■

Debugging

Debugging is a very important part of software development. Only developers who never make mistakes, or developers that maintain code that has no mistakes, should skip this chapter. For the rest of us use of a debugger is critical to understanding code that isn't working correctly. We won't get into the details of "what is a bug" as this can mean many things to many people. In this section we will simply talk about using the standard IDE tools for examining code. There are many complete books dedicated to the theory of bugs and debugging; some of these are listed in the additional resources in the appendix.

Although the concepts are similar and terminology is consistent, debugging commands, actions, and displays are specific to each IDE. The concepts we talk about in this section apply to most modern IDEs and command-line environments. Similar functionality exists in other IDEs other than the one we use to demonstrate a particular concept.

One of the earliest forms of debugging is also the simplest: output statements to the console. In procedural programming a very common debugging technique was to insert output statements all throughout the code. In some early languages these could be turned on through a compile-time macro definition; the statements would only show up if the program was compiled in "DEBUG" mode. While this was certainly effective there were some glaring problems with this approach. The main problem was that the programmer had to know exactly what to send to the console. The values being printed might look fine, but if the program wasn't correct the programmer had to hunt around for additional information to print. Also, if the output screen was very small and the amount of print statements was large it could be difficult to spot the statement of interest.

Breakpoints

The first weapon in the debugging toolkit is the breakpoint. When debugging an application it will stop program execution at the line where it is set. A breakpoint is commonly represented by a symbol in the margin area of the editor, frequently referred to as the "gutter." In Microsoft Visual Studio the symbol is a red circle, in Eclipse the symbol is a small blue circle. An example of each is shown in Figure 5-1. Other IDEs may use similar symbols to represent breakpoints.

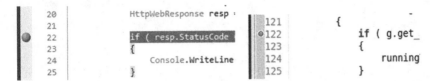

Figure 5-1. *Breakpoint in Visual Studio (left) and Eclipse (right)*

When execution is stopped many things can be examined – the values of in-scope variables, the call-stack, and in some tools an "immediate execution" tool is available for typing ad-hoc expressions. Both IDEs will superimpose an arrow over the current line *before* execution of that line. This is shown in Visual Studio below in Figure 5-2. The arrow is referred to as the "current statement indicator."

```
20          HttpWebResponse resp = (HttpWebResponse)hwr.
21
22          if ( resp.StatusCode == HttpStatusCode.OK )
23          {
24              Console.WriteLine("The site exists");
25          }
```

Figure 5-2. *Execution stopped at breakpoint*

If we place our cursor over any of the variables that are in scope a popup will appear with the variable's value, allowing very quick inspection of the variable. Also, let's look at the some other windows that open, namely the "Locals" window and the "Immediate" window. These are both shown in Figure 5-3.

Locals				Immediate Window
Name	Value	Type		?resp.StatusCode == HttpStatusCode.OK
◊ this	{ConsoleTest.HttpReqRespTest}	Console		true
⊞ ◊ hwr	{System.Net.HttpWebRequest}	System.!		
⊞ ◊ resp	{System.Net.HttpWebResponse}	System.!		

Locals | Watch   Call Stack | Immediate Window

Figure 5-3. *Debugging windows in Visual Studio*

The "Locals" window shows all the variables that are in-scope at the breakpoint's level. In this case there are only three, two of which are .NET Framework objects. Clicking the "+" sign next to each object will allow for inspection of the object's property values. In the "Immediate" window an expression has been typed and the resultant value shown. To see the value of the expression in Visual Studio the expression should be preceded by a question mark. Hence ?resp.StatusCode == HttpStatusCode.OK is a Boolean expression which results in the value of true. Note that variables can also be assigned values in the immediate window if the question mark is omitted; the syntax for that is the same as for any expression.

The two windows not in focus in Figure 5-3 are the "Watch" window and the "Call Stack" window. Whereas the Locals window shows the value of all the in-scope variables, the Watch window allows for narrowing the focus to only specified variables. In cases where there are dozens of variables instead of only three as above this can be extremely helpful in narrowing the focus. The Call Stack window shows each function from the entry point (main() in many languages) down to the current level. This information can be useful to examine if it seems like the breakpoint is being hit unexpectedly. Tracing upward from the current function will show the current caller, the current caller's caller, etc. This will be examined later in the "Stack Trace" section.

By default execution will stop every time the breakpoint is reached. However there may be instances where this type of behavior doesn't work. For instance, if the breakpoint is in the middle of a large loop, stopping every time through may not be necessary. Breakpoints can be made "conditional" by setting a stop condition.

▪ **Note**   The Express Editions of Visual Studio, except for C++, do not allow for conditional breakpoints. All paid versions of Visual Studio allow for conditional breakpoints and will be the same as seen in the following screen snippets, which are taken from Visual C++ 2010 Express Edition.

The symbols for breakpoints in both IDEs are shown in Figure 5-1. Right-clicking on the breakpoint symbol in Visual Studio will launch the context menu in Figure 5-4 – the conditional options are outlined. From this dialog each choice will launch a dialog for setting specifics on each option.

Figure 5-4. *Visual Studio breakpoint menu*

A summary of each option is given in the table below.

Menu Option	Summary
Location...	A summary of the breakpoint's current location, specified by filename and line number.
Condition...	Specify a condition to evaluate with an expression. If the condition is true execution will stop at the breakpoint. Another option is if the value of the expression changes after it is initially evaluated execution will stop.
Hit Count...	Specify a number that will cause execution to stop when the number of hits on the break point 1) is equal to that number 2) is equal to a multiple of that number 3) is greater than that number
Filter...	Specify the breakpoint is only valid on a particular machine, process, or thread.
When Hit...	Allows for the breakpoint to continue executing and print a message to the console, essentially becoming a "tracepoint". Pre-defined macros allow for information such as process ID and thread ID to be included along with variable values.
Edit Labels...	Assigns a label to a breakpoint. This is purely metadata that allows for grouping similar breakpoints in the Breakpoint window, or searching for all breakpoints with a common label, etc.

In Eclipse, right-clicking on the breakpoint and selecting "Breakpoint Properties..." will launch the dialog shown in Figure 5-5. Notice that there are many of the same options available as discussed above. The "Filtering" tab, not highlighted in Figure 5-5, is used for restricting threads by thread ID. Also note that in Eclipse, when a breakpoint is reached, the IDE will switch to the "Debug" perspective, which has views for variables, expressions, etc. These are very similar to the Visual Studio tabs shown above in Figure 5-3.

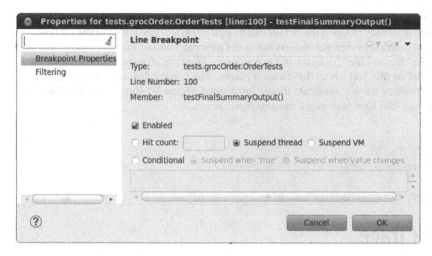

Figure 5-5. *Eclipse breakpoint properties dialog*

Stepping

While being able to break on a specific line and examine the state of the program is extremely useful, another critical debugging activity is stepping through code one line at a time. Once a breakpoint is hit and code execution has stopped, there are several options for continuing the program. The most basic is to simply resume execution; the program will start executing again and continue on until another breakpoint is reached.

Figure 5-6 shows the debug menu bars for both Microsoft Visual Studio and Eclipse. Notice the three buttons on the right side of each image have a similar icon. From left to right these are "step into", "step over", and "step out of" ("step return" in Eclipse). Note that these buttons also have function-key shortcuts, such as F11, F10, and shift-F10 for Visual Studio. "Step over" will simply execute the line of code, whether a simple statement or a method call, and move to the next line. There is also the option to "step into" a method, which will stop the execution at the first line inside of the called method. Note that if the method doesn't have debug information, such as a system or third-party library call, it may not be possible to step into it. Once inside the method stepping may continue a line at a time and can even go into other methods. At any time inside of a method, choosing "step out of" will run to the end of the method and stop at the next line after the method call.

Figure 5-6. *Debug menu bars for Visual Studio (left) and Eclipse (right)*

There are other useful ways to control the execution path during debugging. If the execution is already stopped the cursor can be placed on any line ahead of the current statement indicator. From the context menu the user can choose "Run to Cursor" (Visual Studio) or "Run to Line" (Eclipse) and execution will execute all statements between the current debug line and where the cursor is placed. The current line indicator can also be moved around if some statements should be skipped. Figure 5-7 shows both the "Run to Cursor" and "Set Next Statement" context menu items.

| ✦≣ | Run To Cursor | Ctrl+F10 |
| ➡ | Set Next Statement | Ctrl+Shift+F10 |

Figure 5-7. *Current statement options*

Stack Trace

As mentioned earlier around Figure 5-3, the Call Stack window in Visual Studio contains a representation of function calls that have been made as the code is being executed. This can of limited usefulness while stepping through code because in general that is done in a relatively controlled way. A more informative use for examining the call stack is during an unexpected exception; tracing the stack in this manner will help isolate where the exception was thrown from.

In the code shown in Listing 5-1, an attempt is made to connect to a MySql database. All the data processing code has been removed from the snippet and the database taken offline so that the connection will fail. Notice the catch block of code; it uses the StackTrace property of the MySqlException object to detail where the exception happened. The resulting printout is shown in Figure 5-8.

Listing 5-1. Using the StackTrace property in .NET

```
MySqlConnection conn = new MySqlConnection(strConnection);
MySqlCommand cmd = new MySqlCommand("Select * from customers");

cmd.Connection = conn;
try
{
    conn.Open();
    // code not related to connection failure removed
}
catch (MySqlException mse)
{
    Console.WriteLine("Error while connecting to the
                      database!");
    Console.WriteLine(mse.StackTrace);
}
```

```
Error while connecting to the database!
   at MySql.Data.MySqlClient.MySqlStream.ReadPacket()
   at MySql.Data.MySqlClient.NativeDriver.AuthenticateNew()
   at MySql.Data.MySqlClient.NativeDriver.Open()
   at MySql.Data.MySqlClient.Driver.Open()
   at MySql.Data.MySqlClient.MySqlPool.CreateNewPooledConnection()
   at MySql.Data.MySqlClient.MySqlPool.GetPooledConnection()
   at MySql.Data.MySqlClient.MySqlPool.TryToGetDriver()
   at MySql.Data.MySqlClient.MySqlPool.GetConnection()
   at MySql.Data.MySqlClient.MySqlConnection.Open()
   at ConsoleTest.MySqlSelectTest.DoTest() in C:\projects\dot_net\legacy\Console
Test\MySqlSelectTest.cs:line 43
Test complete.  Press <enter> to return...
```

Figure 5-8. *Result of StackTrace*

The example is a little contrived in that the exception is generate down deep in the MySql source code (ReadPacket()) that is beyond the reach of the client program. However, if this were a real application with dozens of custom assemblies and libraries, the stack trace could help pinpoint misbehaving code in another library. Also, in the next section when logging is discussed, a stack trace could be logged to help pinpoint errors in production code where debugging is not available.

A similar construct is available in the Java Exception class, and in Eclipse the "Call Stack" is shown in both the "Outline View" and the Debug window. These are shown below in Figure 5-9.

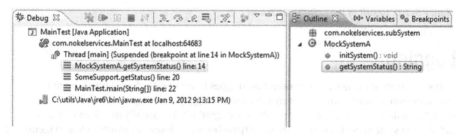

Figure 5-9. *Debug and Outline views in Eclipse*

Actual coding is also similar with the Java Exception class. The portion of code shown in Listing 5-2 results in the print statements shown below in Figure 5-10. Again, this is a contrived exception in very easy to find circumstances, but the principle scales out well to multiple JARs and packages.

Listing 5-2. Stack printing in Java

```
String someStr = "This is a random string";
System.out.println(someStr);
SomeSupport ss = new SomeSupport();
try
{
        ss.getStatus();
}
catch(Exception ex)
{
        System.out.println("Error occurred in subsystem.");
        ex.printStackTrace();
}
```

```
Console 🔲 ⬚ Tasks                 ■ ✖ 🔧 | 🗎 🔝 [🖳] [🖳]  ☐ 🔳 ▼ 📁 ▼ ▭ ☐
<terminated> MainTest [Java Application] C:\utils\Java\jre6\bin\javaw.exe (Jan 9, 2012 9:26:01 PM)
This is a basic Java console app.
This is a random string
java.lang.ArithmeticException: / by zero
        at com.nokelservices.subSystem.MockSystemA.getSystemStatus(MockSystemA.ja
        at com.nokelservices.SomeSupport.getStatus(SomeSupport.java:18)
        at com.nokelservices.MainTest.main(MainTest.java:23)
Error occurred in subsystem.
```

Figure 5-10. *Result of the printStackTrace()*

Logging

Of course, once code goes into production or goes to retail sale, debugging is usually not an option. Symbols and structures used in debugging add significant overhead to an executable and this size and performance degradation is usually not desirable in a production system. So how to aid in identifying bugs and issues in a production system? Logging is the key.

Initially logging consisted of simple statements to a text file via the println method mentioned above. While this was simple and very popular there was seldom a defined format or a consistent structure among applications. Microsoft Windows exposed an API for logging to application and system event logs. While this provided a consistent format for application logging there were often issues accessing these logs for analysis.

Two very popular tools that are of the same family are log4j and log4net; these are supplemental libraries produced by the Apache Software Foundation. These tools allow for writing to many different types of "log files", including text files, databases, email, and more. Syntax for configuration and actual use of the components is very similar, as log4net is a port of the log4j code. There are other ports as well; for C++, JavaScript, and more but those won't be covered here. In the following discussion the term "log4" will be used to denote the discussion applies to both log4net and log4j. In general it should be assumed that when one product is mentioned the same concept applies to the other unless otherwise mentioned.

As these are outside libraries, the first step to including them in a project is to add the correct assembly or JAR file to the project. After inclusion in the project the logging must be configured. In a project using log4net this can be accomplished with a separate XML configuration file or a custom configuration section within the app.config or web.config file. In log4j both an XML file and a .properties file are supported. The example presented below shows XML configuration snippets for log4net; the concepts, property names, and other options should be very similar between log4net and log4j no matter how they are configured. Many of the items mentioned here can be further researched by going to the Apache logging website: http://loging.apache.org.

One of the strengths of using log4 is the separation between programmatic use and declarative definition. Programmatically, a logger object is used to send statements to the log file. The logger is usually an interface variable and doesn't know or care about the actual log. The snippets in Listing 5-3 show the declaration of the log variable and an example of its use. By convention a single log variable is defined in each class where logging is desired; a unique identifier string or a type name is used to label statements from this logger in the log.

A core concept in log4 is the appender. This can also be thought of as the logging target – where the log statements are written. There are several pre-defined appenders in each product; examples of these are the file appender, event log appender, and console appender. In the example shown in Figure 5-14 below a RollingFileAppender is used; this type of file appender will rotate files based on certain configuration parameters.

Note that the first part of Figure 5-14, <configSections>, is the method of defining a custom configuration section in a .NET configuration file, it is NOT related to the actual definition of the appender in the log4 framework.

Listing 5-3. Declaring and using a logger

```
public class MyClass
{
    protected static ILog log =
        LogManager.GetLogger(typeof(MySqlSelectTest));
    // other source here...
    // In any method of the class:
    log.Info("Connection String to MySQL db: " +
            strConnection);
}
```

Listing 5-4. Appender configuration with layout

```
<configSections>
  <section name="log4net"
    type="log4net.Config.Log4NetConfigurationSectionHandler,
              log4net" requirePermission="false"/>
</configSections>
```

```
<log4net>
  <appender name="LogFileAppender"
            type="log4net.Appender.RollingFileAppender">
    <param name="File" value="${LOGS}\consoleLogFile.txt"/>
    <rollingStyle value="Date"/>
    <datePattern value="yyyyMMdd-HH" />
    <layout type="log4net.Layout.PatternLayout">
      <conversionPattern
        value="%d{MM-dd-yyyy::HH:mm:ss} | %-5p %c | %m %n" />
    </layout>
  </appender>
</log4net>
```

In the case of Listing 5-4 the file will role based on a date value and is specifically defined to roll hourly via the datePattern element. Another option would be rolling on size or every program execution. The other parameter of interest is the "File" parameter and its use of the ${LOGS} value; LOGS is a system environment variable specifying the logging directory. This keeps the logging directory from being hard-coded into the configuration file.

The final key to producing a log file is the <layout> element in the appender. This element defines the content and format of the information written to the logging destination. In many respects it is similar to the string formatting functionality available in modern programming languages. Characters which will be replaced by content are prefaced with the percent (%) sign and optional formatting and spacing can be applied to each. Each character also signifies a special piece of content; the full listing of which is present in the documentation. The table below summarizes the escape characters present in the above conversion pattern.

Character	Meaning
%d	The date when the log entry is written – formatting of the date specified by the following {} content.
%p	The level of entry. Levels are INFO, ERROR, etc.
%c	The name of the logger.
%m	The message provided to the logger.
%n	A newline constant.

Once these pieces are in place, logs will be written as specified. After several runs of the test program the log directory will look like Figure 5-11. Notice there is one log file for each hour, just as was specified; the date format we specified is added to the filename when the file is rolled. Only the current file has the filename that was specified in the configuration.

Name	Size	Date modified
consoleLogFile.txt	1 KB	6/5/2011 1:05 AM
consoleLogFile.txt20110604-23	2 KB	6/4/2011 11:51 PM
consoleLogFile.txt20110604-21	2 KB	6/4/2011 9:29 PM
consoleLogFile.txt20110603-22	3 KB	6/3/2011 10:59 PM

Figure 5-11. *Several log files based on the hour*

A sample of the output is shown in Listing 5-5. Each line follows the format that was specified in the configuration with expanded content. The inter-line wrapping is caused by the limitations of the textbox; in the actual log file each statement is a single line.

Listing 5-5. Sample log statements

```
06-05-2011::01:05:12 | INFO  ConsoleTest.ConsoleTest_1 | Starting the test
for the ConsoleTest.MySqlSelectTest class
06-05-2011::01:05:12 | INFO  ConsoleTest.MySqlSelectTest | Connection
String to MySQL db: Database=test;Data Source=localhost;User
Id=user;Password=password
06-05-2011::01:05:13 | INFO  ConsoleTest.MySqlSelectTest | Connected to
database, issuing command 'Select ID, name, address from customers'
06-05-2011::01:05:13 | INFO  ConsoleTest.MySqlSelectTest | Recordset
returned with 3 columns.
```

One final note about logging. This example follows the same pattern as all others in the book - it is kept necessarily simple due to space considerations. The next step would be use multiple levels in the program code; possible levels include DEBUG, WARN, ERROR, and FATAL, which are matched by similar functions in the log interface (log.debug(), log.warn(), etc.) This could also be matched by defining multiple appenders, each one being filtered to handle a particular level to a different destination. Full discussion of this is beyond the scope of this book; please refer to the online documentation for further examples.

Summary

Debugging is a very import part of software development. It has come a long way since the use of simple output statements; modern IDEs allow for breakpoints, variable inspection, stepping, and execution manipulation to help the programmer monitor execution. Despite our best efforts during development, bugs will still manage to creep into software. Use of logging tools will help to monitor program execution once it has left an environment easily accessible to the debugger. Log4 products were discussed and highlighted but there are many additional products out there. At the time of this writing the log4net product had not been updated in over 4 years; log4j has only had a minor release in the past 4 years. While these are very stable and practical some may not be comfortable with such infrequently updated open source projects; other logging products are available. In the Microsoft space NLog and the Microsoft Enterprise Library are actively developed. If none of these are suitable, custom logging can be developed from scratch. Whichever road is chosen, a combination of thorough debugging and judicious logging can greatly improve software quality and the use of both is very common in professional software development.

CHAPTER 6

■ ■ ■

Development Methodologies and SDLC

Most software development organizations make use of a standard set of practices when developing software. This is commonly known as the software development life cycle (SDLC) and the method used to implement the life cycle loosely fall into two categories: Waterfall and Agile. We will briefly discuss each of these methods but acknowledge that there are many different variations and combinations of techniques. We cannot cover all the variations, but hope to cover the main points of each such that the variations are simple modifications of what is here, not a radical first step into the world of applied methodologies.

Waterfall

The waterfall model of software development is a method that originated from other well defined processes at the time; construction, manufacturing, and other classical engineering disciplines. These are all examples of sequential process control where each step in the process was well-defined and all pieces had a well understood order of completion. Each step needs to be completed before moving on to the next phase. The picture in Figure 6-1 shows a graphical representation of the steps involved.

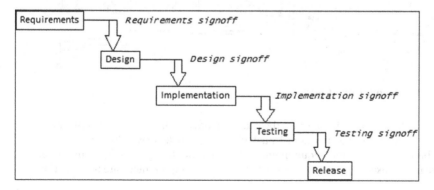

Figure 6-1. *Typical Waterfall method steps*

Unfortunately for software developers the waterfall methodology is typically documentation-heavy. This is commonly due to the many separate teams involved in the overall development and the need for approvals to be recorded before moving to the next stage in the process.

Before moving into the design phase the requirements must be fully documented by the business users and acknowledged to be a complete list of desired functionality (Requirements will be discussed more in Chapter 8: Software Requirements). Before moving to implementation the technical team must design the system to meet the requirements. This design is usually reviewed by technical management, business user management, and project management to ensure that all requirements are met in the design. Often times a "Gap "Analysis" is done as part of this stage; it will state the requirements that are not addressed by the design. The final design document will cite both the original requirements and the gap analysis document.

■ **Note**   In this discussion the term "business users" is used to describe those who produce the requirements. For an internal application this may be another department such as accounting or human resources. For a retail product this may be a sales team or product development team which has a vision for the retail product.

During this process one or more Gantt charts may be constructed in a project management tool such as Microsoft Project. There may be one for the overall project maintained by the project manager and the development team may have one specific to the coding effort. These charts detail the work to be done and keep track of the dependencies between items and are constructed at the start of the project. They also track status such as completed items and percent complete for in-progress tasks along with due dates and resources. Charts are updated in regularly scheduled project meetings that typically involve the entire team and management. A very simplified Gantt chart is shown in Figure 6-2.

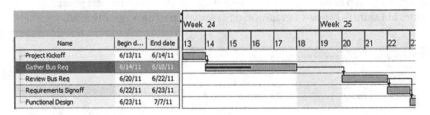

Figure 6-2. Simple Gantt Chart

Once development is complete the code can move to the testing and verification phase. This testing is typically done by a dedicated testing team who has prepared test cases based on the original requirement documents and their knowledge of the system. This team will exercise the system ensuring that all the requirements are met and the system behaves correctly. Depending on the product, type of project, and skill of the testers different types of testing can be done. The table below gives a summary of testing terms and their description.

Type of Testing	Description
Regression Testing	If the new code is an upgrade to existing code the entire system will be tested to ensure the new functionality did not change any existing functionality.
User Acceptance Testing	This tests that the new software meets the requirements laid out in the business user's requirements document. Business users usually participate in this testing or oversee the test scripts to ensure they are complete.
Integration Testing	If the system under test interacts with other systems this testing ensures compatibility.
Black Box Testing	The testers will not know anything about the internals of the system and simply label tests as "Pass/Fail."
White Box Testing	The testers may know some details about the inner workings of the system and in addition to "Pass/Fail" may be able to give insight about what is causing errors.
Performance Testing	The system is load-tested to determine its throughput, processing, or scalability performance.

Once testing is complete the system can be released to the users – either into production if an internal product or to the public if it is a retail product. At this stage maintenance begins and any bug fixes or possibly minor enhancements may be done.

So the question arises "What if the requirements change after the requirements document is finalized?" Different organizations may handle this differently based on the extent of the change, but in most cases there is a "change request" process that is followed. This essentially is the entire process followed again but only for this single item. So the statement of change would be reviewed and approved by the business users, the change in design would be analyzed and documented by the developers, and the testers would be made aware of this change.

Because of the inflexible nature of this process, several modifications of the process have taken place to make the waterfall model more compatible with the pace of software and hardware innovation. One of the popular modifications resulted in the term "iterfall" which describes the process of performing waterfall development but on a much smaller scale, breaking the project down into phases. During each phase the same waterfall steps are followed and the entire process is done in an iterative fashion. This may also be combined with the "Big Design Up Front" model. In this model the entire project is designed up front but releases are planned in stages with each release following a waterfall-type documentation and development procedure.

Agile

In contrast to the regimented stages of the waterfall method, agile software development methodologies attempt to address the fact that changes not only happen but can be expected. This is an example of empirical process control (Schwaber, 2004) and rather than relying on detailed documentation from the outset and a standard repeatable process, frequent feedback and adaptation is used to steer the design and development towards the end software goal. One of the most popular agile frameworks is Scrum; it will be described in this section. Many of the concepts here are outlined in more detail in the book *AGILE PROJECT MANAGEMENT WITH SCRUM* (Schwaber, 2004); this section is an overview and should be supplemented with additional resources listed in the appendix.

Scrum is a framework for managing the delivery of software on a short and predictable iterative schedule. Instead of producing a large design up front and then implementing the entire product in one big bang, the goal of Scrum is to deliver some piece of working functionality every development cycle. In Scrum terms, a development cycle is known as a "sprint." It may take several sprints to complete a fully functional release, but the key is that each sprint produces *something* a customer can test. Below we will describe both the new terms and the rules of Scrum and discuss how the overall process differs from waterfall. Many of these terms and ideals are common to the agile methodologies and this discussion should carry over to other methods.

The first set of terms to describe deal with the people who participate in the project. Rather than have a large hierarchical structure of teams and sub-teams and managers for each, Scrum attempts to keep the organization simple. There are only three roles in Scrum; the product owner, the team, and the Scrum Master. These roles work together to define and implement the product.

The Product Owner is the person who has an interest in having the software built. Typically this is a business person who needs a new piece of software, or a product development person who is responsible for creating a new retail product. This person possesses the vision and desire for a piece of software but doesn't have the ability to write it. In Scrum, the product owner is solely responsible for creating the "requirements", organizing and prioritizing them, and evaluating the software at each sprint. During the sprint the product owner only provides input if asked by the development team or Scrum Master.

The Scrum Master is the role which is analogous to a project manager in the waterfall method. However in Scrum the responsibility is that of a facilitator rather than a traditional manager. The Scrum Master coordinates and runs the required meetings of the Scrum process (described below) and also works to remove any roadblocks during development. They also enforce the rules of Scrum which involve certain time limits on the different meetings, speaking restrictions, and coordination.

One of the different things about the team in Scrum is that they are self-organizing. This doesn't mean necessarily that the team has no structure; it means that during the sprints no one manages the team except for the team itself. The Scrum Master interacts with the team daily and may enforce the rules of Scrum but typically doesn't interfere with the actual work done by the team. Team members may have many different talents such as developer, technical writer, tester, SQL specialist, etc., but there is no standard team structure in scrum – only what is necessary to implement the functionality for a given sprint. In addition, the arrangement of a cross-functional team improves communication and accountability.

A team may ask for outside input during a sprint. It may need clarification from the product owner on a particular topic, or it may ask the Scrum Master to help resolve an issue the team is having, internal or external to the team. For example, if the team needs to use the services of another group and that group is slow to respond, the team may ask the Scrum Master to escalate the problem if it is blocking progress.

It has been mentioned several times, but now we will further define one of the most important new terms – the "sprint." As defined above, a sprint is a development cycle that produces at least one piece of workable and verifiable functionality. Each sprint is equal length, typically thirty calendar days. Organizations may decide on a different length but there are pros and cons to going much shorter or much longer. Shorter and there may not be enough time to produce a workable feature; longer and the risk is not responding quickly enough to a product owner's change. With few exceptions the sprint length should be kept constant for the entire project.

To start each sprint the Scrum Master facilitates a "Sprint Planning Meeting" to bring together the product owner and development team. This is a time-boxed meeting and cannot go beyond the allotted time. It is recommended that this meeting be no more than eight hours and split into two equal halves. This meeting produces two things (and introduces two new terms!): a product backlog and a sprint backlog.

A product backlog is a list of requirement-like statements about what the finished product will do. This list is produced and owned by the product owner and is normally expressed in terms the owner understands. Hence, instead of "requirements" these are often referred to as "stories." In the first half of the sprint planning meeting, the team works with the product owner to prioritize and then clarify these stories. The team also works to estimate how much work each story represents, using a "point system", and estimates how many "story points" they can complete during the next sprint (more on project progress later). Since the stories are prioritized by the product owner the team generally selects a subset of stories that are the highest priority. The selected items are used as input to the second half of the meeting; planning the sprint backlog.

During the second half of the sprint planning meeting the selected story items are analyzed and expanded out into details by the team. This forms the sprint backlog and details all items in the sprint that will cover all the stories chosen from the product backlog. This list is owned and managed by the team so it may be expressed in more technical terms. At the end of the meeting all the items in the sprint backlog should be detailed, estimated and assigned.

There are many methods of organizing the product and spring backlogs items. Some teams may use spreadsheet software or other special item tracking or project management software. However, since the emphasis in Agile is for lightweight documentation, many teams simply use index cards or sticky notes with a story summary (for the product backlog) or a more detailed item (for the sprint backlog), one item per card. These are easy to quickly edit and share in meetings, and easy to keep track of in physical locations. An example is detailed in (Kniberg, 2007) in which cards are physically taped to the project board in the team room. These are highly visible and the project status is open and transparent.

Once into the sprint, the team and Scrum Master interact in a daily meeting known as the Daily Scrum. This meeting is no longer than 15 minutes and should be held at roughly the same time every day. During this meeting only one team member is allowed to talk at a time, directly in response to the Scrum Master's simple questions:

1. What have you done since the last meeting?

2. What will you do before the next meeting?

3. Are there any impediments to you doing your work?

The Scrum Master may record these answers to keep a running log of work done and work remaining. Any impediments should be resolved by the Scrum Master; the team concentrates on completing the tasks in the sprint backlog.

So how is progress measured? Completed items are plotted against time in a graph known as a "burndown chart." This allows for comparison of the number of items remaining versus time and can be done on a sprint level and the overall project level. Backlog items or sprint story points are always on the vertical graph; it may be easier to visualize story points. The horizontal axis is time, either number of sprints for the project burndown, or days for a sprint burndown. For a sprint the progress is tracked after each daily scrum. So for example, if the team committed to 32 story points for a particular sprint the first plot point would be day one of the sprint with a marker on the vertical axis at 32. After the next daily scrum, if the team completes 3 story points the marker would be at 29. For day three, two completed points would put the marker at 27, and so on. Ideally on day 30 (or the last day of the sprint) the marker is at zero, meaning that all work was completed as of the last day of the sprint. A sample sprint burndown chart is shown below in Figure 6-3. A little over halfway through does the sprint appear to be on track?

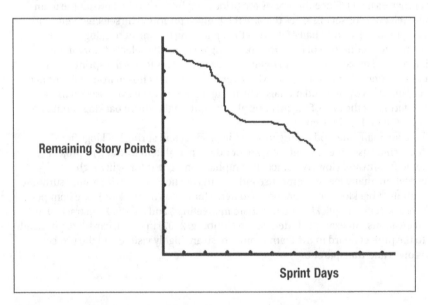

Figure 6-3. Sample Sprint Burndown Chart

After a few sprints the team should have a good feel for its "velocity", or the typical number of story points the team can handle in a sprint. This should give the Scrum Master a better feel for project time frames and this can then be communicated to the product owner via the project burndown chart. As stated above, the ideal burndown would roughly follow a 45-degree downward sloped line. Deviation one way or the other would be a clue that estimation is incorrect and needs to be adjusted in future sprints.

At the end of each sprint the working functionality is demonstrated to the product owner in the "sprint review" meeting. This meeting is also time-boxed and is for the sole purpose of gathering feedback on the just-completed stories. This frequent feedback is crucial to agile development and serves several purposes:

1. Lets the product owner see that progress is being made.

2. Lets the product owner see each set of functionality as it is being completed rather than one "big bang" at the end.

3. If the team was somehow completely wrong on their implementation of a story the feedback is given while fresh in everyone's mind and no more than a sprint-length of time has been lost.

4. Gives the product owner flexibility to reassess priorities frequently.

Another meeting that the team has at the end of a sprint is the "sprint retrospective." This is only for the team and the Scrum Master to attend; the purpose is to review the sprint and discuss the team's operation. What the team did right, wrong, or could start doing to improve efficiency are all topics for the discussion. Early in the project this meeting is generally held after each sprint. Further into the project this meeting may change to only by request or after a certain number of sprints.

Note that Scrum does not prescribe how to do the actual development. Although test driven development, discussed in the section "Test Driven Development (TDD)", is very popular, SCRUM does not require any one form of actual coding to be employed. Simply that daily scrums, sprint planning and review, backlogs and burn-downs are performed. Extreme programming (XP), is often combined with Scrum, a very good description of which is in "*Scrum and XP from the Trenches*" (Kniberg, 2007). A brief summary of XP is given in the next section. Also, in some large organizations where the waterfall method is firmly entrenched in the project management structure, Scrum is sometimes used by the development team with some role modifications. Descriptions of all of these are beyond the scope of this book, but what is outlined above is the suggested outline for Scrum; real-world adaptions abound.

Extreme Programming

Many practices that are part of extreme programming (XP) have already been discussed but not formally identified as part of XP. For example, test driven development and refactoring both play an important role in XP, but both can also be practiced outside of XP on their own. Also, similar terms are used in XP and Scrum, but XP mainly applies to the coding team whereas Scrum encompasses many roles and arguably falls under the category of a project management framework. This section will briefly explain how these previously described development techniques are woven into the discipline of extreme programming within our Scrum project and what additional techniques apply. Many excellent resources are available to further explain XP both within and without Scrum; a few are listed in the appendix.

At the point where the development team is ready to start coding the items in the sprint backlog, XP can be applied. As highlighted earlier this would involve test-driven development at the actual coding level. However, XP prescribes a collaborative programming arrangement known as pair-programming, where two programmers work in tandem on a single workstation.

How does *that* work? It seems strange, but can actually be very stressful and very productive at the same time. It is similar to a brainstorming session in that ideas can be bounced off of a peer, and the code being written is also be scrutinized by a partner with the same end goal. Although it takes some getting used to in terms of how much and what kind of feedback to share, the end goal is often cleaner, better code in a shorter amount of time.

One person is at the keyboard (sometimes referred to as the driver) and is concerned with the actual typing of the code. The other person (the navigator) is responsible for non-coding strategic items and team practices. These responsibilities can range from making sure a unit test is written first to remembering the correct number of arguments for a certain API call to ensuring that typos won't result in compile errors. The navigator can also think strategically and identify if a certain function may need to be more generic or validate input from an interfacing system. This falls under the realm of refactoring; this can also relate to how the code fits into the overall program.

The driver/navigator arrangement is not necessarily rigid for any particular programming session. If the driver is having difficulty with a certain construct or has been hit with an episode of "brain freeze", it may be time to switch. Something along the lines of "Can I drive for a minute?" may signal a good time to pass the keyboard and switch roles. This keeps both partners fresh and thinking both at the code level and at a higher strategic level with near-instantaneous feedback.

In addition to TDD, refactoring, and pair programming, here are some other tenets of XP with a brief explanation and rationale for each.

Collective code ownership – the entire source code base is open to everyone and anyone can change any piece. This is both for rapid response and for limiting risk; a specialized piece of code known only to one person is a large liability should the person leave the company or a critical bug appear just after that person started their two week hike on the Appalachian Trail.

Coding standard – the code is open to everyone, therefore a common standard should be employed. This helps while pair programming, refactoring, and in maintenance.

Daily builds/continuous integration – XP relies on TDD and refactoring to ensure smooth integration of new code. This can be further ensured by enforcing that all checked-in code compiles smoothly, and doubly-ensured by enforcing that all checked in code results in 100% success in the unit tests.

Sustainable productivity – work time should be constant and relatively close to a "normal" forty-hour week. This prevents burn-out, but more importantly the team will get very good at estimating how much can be accomplished in a "normal" week. This should improve the entire process of estimating and delivering on-time and on-budget.

Distributed Teams

In Scrum and XP the ideal arrangement is for the entire team to be able to physically meet every day for the daily scrum and to be close to support pair programming and other forms of near-instant feedback. As discussed later in Appendix A teams are becoming increasingly distributed in nature. So how does this affect Scrum?

There are several ways to deal with distributed team members. Some teams may rely on online tools or publicly shared folders for housing documentation. Collaborative meeting software can be used so share plans and discuss backlogs; video conferencing and bridge lines can also be used for communication.

Even with these collaboration technologies, distributed team members frequently create more work for Scrum Master. Even if that is simply more time on email, chat, or the phone, many professionals argue that the ability to walk directly to someone's desk to discuss an issue face to face increases productivity and team cohesiveness.

Distributed Version Control

As discussed briefly in Chapter 1: Version Control, the impact of distributed teams has also had an effect on version control systems. While many of the concepts of editing, committing, merging, and conflicts still exist, distributed teams, especially smaller teams that may be geographically dispersed and have no dedicated intranet, will often use distributed version control systems such as GIT, Mercurial, or Veracity. The following paragraphs describe how distributed systems differ in theory from the previously described centralized system.

Remember that SVN and other centralized version control systems (VCSs) normally operate with a central repository from which users check out files, edit them, and check them back in. Also recall that when checking a file in the system will ensure the edited file is based on the latest repository version. If not the user must first merge the latest version *from* the repository with the local changes, then commit the merged file to the repository.

Distributed VCSs are based on the theory that multiple copies of the entire repository exist and that each copy is a complete and valid entity. Working with this local repository is similar to working with a centralized one; files are edited and checked in when complete; tags and braches can be used; branches can be merged back into the main line of code. All of these changes are tracked locally by the VCS and a file's complete history is maintained in this local repository. This means that a network is not required to take advantage of versioning, history, and other features of a VCS.

Another contrast with centralized VCSs comes when sharing with other developers. Instead of "checking out" files from a central server, the entire repository is "cloned" and becomes a new, separate instance that the new user may now operate on. These repositories may change independent of the other. To sync the two repositories each local user will either "push" changes to the remote repository or "pull" changes from the remote repository. Files are merged during these operations and the repositories can remain in sync.

In practice, large organizations that use distributed VCSs may use them in a way that approaches the centralized model. That is, a "master" copy of the repository exists and serves as the source for the official build and release process. Users may "clone" this master copy when starting development and then "push" their changes back when complete. The "master" is commonly integrated with the enterprise CI system. Again, the advantage is that users can be disconnected from this "master" and still take advantage of all the advanced aspects of the system.

Many of the distributed systems have GUI clients, shell extensions, or IDE plug-ins that simplifies working with these repositories. For example, the TortoiseSVN Windows® Explorer extension discussed earlier also has a port for GIT. The difference is that the additional functionality of cloning, pushing, and pulling are wired in to allow for working with remote repositories.

Summary

Development and project methodologies are used in most software development. In this section we've discussed basic versions of the two most prevalent: waterfall and agile. Keep in mind that this section was a pretty high-level overview; continued training and even certification in your chosen methodology, if available, is encouraged. Also there is no way to cover the numerous modifications and adaptations of these methodologies. Regardless, by knowing the basics discussed above the reader should be able to go into any software development team, spend a few minutes talking with the current staff about the method, identify whether it is waterfall-like or agile-like, and proceed from there. Some factors of XP may seem a little strange, but remembering the goal is increased productivity and code quality is crucial.

Distributed team may require slight adaptions to the methodologies discussed here. Version control systems have also been affected by distributed teams. Although in general the concepts are very similar, multiple repositories often seem strange at first. But the features and power given to individual developers who may not always be connected to the network is usually worth the learning curve.

■ ■ ■

CHAPTER 7

Design Patterns and Architecture

The term "Design Pattern" in software engineering refers to a known arrangement of software components that solves a particular problem. These structures provide both a known terminology and known implementation such that once the particular problem is identified, the known structure can be applied. One of the earliest formal definitions of software patterns is detailed in *Design Patterns: Elements of Reusable Object-Oriented Software* (Gamma et al., 1994), sometimes referred to as the "Gang of Four" (GoF) because of the four original authors. That work has been the inspiration for several updated and language-specific books. In this section we will briefly cover a few GoF patterns to demonstrate the terminology and as an introduction to thinking in patterns. We will then talk about some of the more prevalent patterns in use today in the highly distributed world. Finally we will cover some architectural patterns that are common in large distributed systems and hardware farms that are built for performance and resiliency.

Pattern Examples

As mentioned above, the GoF book was one of the first publications to establish formal definitions for software pattern designs. Many of the patterns had been in use by software developers for some time, but to formalize their definition and structure brought clarity and common terminology and allowed for a common set of patterns to be expanded upon. In this section we will look at three of the more obvious patterns as a way of introduction: observer, facade, and singleton. These are examples of behavioral, structural, and creational patterns respectively.

The Observer Pattern (Behavioral)

Also known as "publish-subscribe", the observer pattern consists of two components. One entity known as the "subject" will expose an event that other entities, known as "observers", can register to listen for and receive notification when the event happens. The observers can also un-register when they are no longer interested in being notified of the event.

In most implementations the observer implements an interface that is specified by the subject. The diagram in Figure 7-1 shows the classes and interface with the bare necessities. The code snippet in the figure also shows a typical implementation of the subject's method to notify the registered observers. The method simply loops over the list of observers calling the interface method on each.

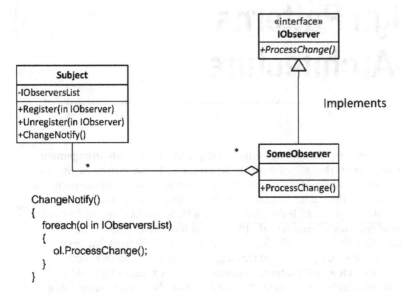

```
ChangeNotify()
{
    foreach(ol in IObserversList)
    {
        ol.ProcessChange();
    }
}
```

Figure 7-1. *Observer structure diagram*

Optionally, if the subject is to provide information to the observer(s) it may also implement an interface so that the observers can use that interface to communicate with the subject. The subject interface typically exposes additional internal information so that after a notification, an observer may call back into the subject for further status.

Practical examples of this pattern abound. Chat rooms, instant messaging, live weather updates; all of these are examples of an observer who registers with a subject to be notified of changes within the subject.

The Façade Pattern (Structural)

The façade pattern's purpose in life is to simplify the external interface to a complex internal system. This allows the internal system to be modularized and broken into independent components with other patterns for performance, testing, or additional purposes. A client of the system, using the façade, has a much simpler interface.

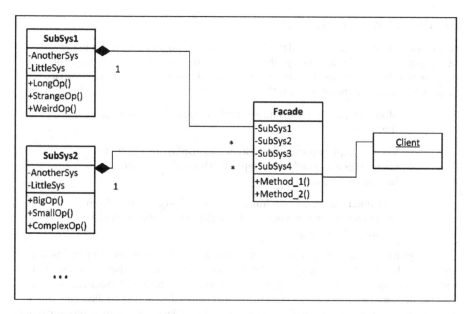

Figure 7-2. *Facade pattern structure*

The client is only presented with Method_1() or Method_2() and is blissfully unaware of the complexity of each call. Each call can make use of one or more of the defined subsystems and as long as the intent of the method doesn't change the client won't need to update any references as the subsystems change.

The Singleton Pattern (Creational)

Singletons ensure that there is only one instance of their particular class created. In languages such as Java and C#, this is accomplished through a combination of a private constructor and static Create() or getInstance() method. Rather than create a new instance each time, this method returns a reference to an existing instance such that all clients share a single instance. This would be useful for security gateway applications or classes that are extremely resource-heavy and would be expensive to continually create and destroy.

Enterprise Patterns: MVC and Inversion of Control

While most patterns are very important, there are two that are particularly important and prevalent in distributed and/or enterprise environments. These are the Model-View-Controller pattern and the Inversion of Control pattern and lend themselves very well to component-based development. They will be discussed in the following sections.

Model-View-Controller

One of the oldest patterns is called the Model-View-Controller (MVC). Originally developed in the Smalltalk language this pattern is extremely prevalent today, especially with the proliferation of web and mobile applications. Before a diagram is shown a definition of each component is as follows:

- Model –represents the data and optionally the business logic of the system.

- View –accepts inputs to the system and displays results to the client. This is typically some type of GUI but doesn't necessarily have to be a human interface.

- Controller –accepts input from the view and requests data from the model; determines actions for both the view and model based on programmed logic.

The primary advantage of this pattern is that the view is separated from the model and hence the view can be changed without impacting the model. Also, the model and controller can be tested and verified without a view via unit tests and mock controllers. This is extremely beneficial in the current atmosphere of distributed applications where a mobile phone application, a web application, and a desktop client can all be connected to the same data model. The controller, sitting in front of the model, can analyze each request and optimize the response based on the client.

Graphically the pattern looks like Figure 7-3.

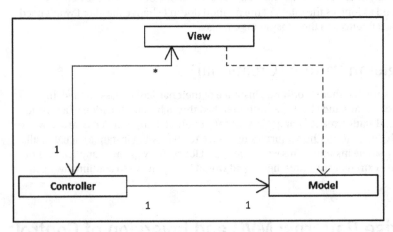

Figure 7-3. *Model-View-Controller (MVC) pattern*

Some items to notice about the pattern:

1. The controller can support many views.

2. The view has a dependency on the model but the model doesn't depend on any other components.

3. The controller communicates directly with the view and the model.

An example of this may be a simple phone list. For a desktop application the entire phone list could be returned based on the assumption that the client is on the local network. For a mobile phone application the list might be returned in chunks to make better use of bandwidth. The controller would be the component making that bandwidth judgment and determining how the interaction happens between the model and the view. The view has to know what pieces of data to show (last name, first name, area code, work or cell, etc.) but the model has no knowledge of the presentation.

Inversion of Control

Inversion of Control (IoC), also known as Dependency Injection (DI), is a very important pattern for systems that have many distributed components and must be tested separately. It extends the concept of "separation of duties" with the addition of classes that are creation agnostic.

Simply put, if a class makes use of the services of another class, the consumer of the service should NOT create instances of the provider of the service. Rather, the provider should define an abstraction (typically an interface) and the consumer should use that interface.

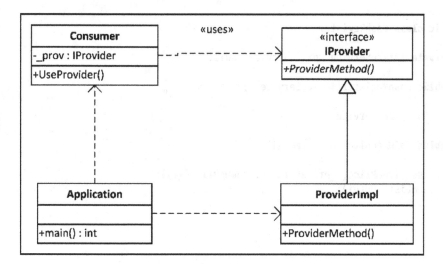

Figure 7-4. Inversion of Control pattern

The consumer can maintain a reference to the interface and can use any class that implements that interface. During testing, "mock" objects can implement the interface, allowing for testing against a known set of values returned by the mock implementation.

The term "inversion of control" comes about because the consumer doesn't control the creation of dependent objects; those are created externally and fed to the consumer. The implementation of passing the external provider is known as "dependency injection" and can be implemented in one of three ways – constructor injection, setting injection, or method injection. These are explained in the following sections with brief descriptions and code snippets.

Manual Example

Returning to the grocery item example from Chapter 3 the usage of the PriceService class by the CashRegister class can be changed slightly to demonstrate all three methods of injection. In Figure 3-1 a PriceService object is instantiated and passed in to the CashRegister object through the constructor; a basic example of "constructor injection" using a class object. Rather than a dedicated object, an interface IPriceService will be used to keep in line with the above discussion and also to later discuss configured dependency injection with a third-party framework.

In Listing 7-1 there is a very simple interface defined and a very simple CashRegister class to make use of the interface via constructor injection.

Listing 7-1. Interface and Consumer

```
public interface IPriceService
{
    double lookUpPrice(GrocItem gi);
}

public class CashRegister
{
  private IPriceService _priceService =null;

  public CashRegister(IPriceService p)
  {
    this._priceService = p;
  }
  public void AddItem(GrocItem gi)
  {
    gi.set_itemPrice( _priceService.lookUpPrice(gi));
    _itemList.add(gi);
  }
}
```

The program that makes use of the CashRegister then gets to decide what type of price service to use. If running a unit test the price service may be a mock implementation that returns a single known value for each item so that total, tax, and discount logic is easy to verify. For the actual production program the price service may query a database or use a web service to obtain a price. No matter the implementation, the CashRegister only knows to use the IPriceService interface and lookUpPrice method to get a price for an item. Figures 7-6 and 7-7 show examples of the use of mock and actual objects for a unit test and an actual implementation.

Listing 7-2. Testing with a mock object

```
@Test
public void testSubTotal()
{
    IPriceService ps = new MockPriceService();
    CashRegister cr = new CashRegister(ps);

    GrocItem giFood1 = new GrocItem("Burger");
    GrocItem giFood2 = new GrocItem("Bread");

    cr.AddItem(giFood1);
    assertEquals(10.0, cr.CalculateOrderSubTotal());

    cr.AddItem(giFood2);
    assertEquals(20.0, cr.CalculateOrderSubTotal());

}

public class MockPriceService implements IPriceService
{
    @Override
    public double lookUpPrice(GrocItem gi)
    {
        return 10.0;
    }
}
```

Listing 7-3. Another Price Service

```java
public class ConsoleApp
{
  public static void main(String[] args)
  {
    IPriceService ps = new LookupPriceService();
    CashRegister cr = new CashRegister(ps);

    GrocItem gi = new GrocItem("Bread");
    cr.AddItem(gi);

    // ...
  }
}
public class LookupPriceService implements IPriceService
{
  @Override
  public double lookUpPrice(GrocItem gi)
  {
    // Hard coded price lookup table
    String upper = gi.get_itemName().toUpperCase();
    double price = 0.0;

    if ( upper.equals("BURGER") )
    {
      price = 5.0;
    }
    else if (upper.equals("BREAD"))
    {
      price = 2.99;
    }
    // ... More items ...

    return price;
  }
}
```

For the other two types of injection, setter injection and method injection, simple additions to the code will allow for alternate methods of using the interface. Listing 7-4 shows the additional code that would be needed for the CashRegister class to support setter and method injection in addition to constructor injection. For use of setter injection additional checks would also need to be put in place to ensure that _priceService was not null before usage.

Listing 7-4. Code for setter and method injection

```
public class CashRegister
{
  private IPriceService _priceService = null;

  // ... previous declarations not included ...
  public setPriceService(IPriceService p)
  {
    this._priceService = p;
  }
  public void AddItem(GrocItem gi, IPriceService ps)
  {
    gi.set_itemPrice(ps.lookUpPrice(gi));
    _itemList.add(gi);
  }
}
```

Configured Example

While the examples above used manual code to accomplish the injection of the dependent object, many frameworks exist for handling injection automatically via configuration files and class name resolution. One of the more popular frameworks which is available for both Java and .NET is Spring, available at the time of this writing from http://www.springsource.org or http://springframework.net respectively. While beyond the scope of this book to discuss Spring in detail, the idea is that consumers and providers are wired together through configuration files and named instances.

The source code file gets a reference to a desired interface through a named instance; the name is listed in the configuration file and associated with a particular class that implements the desired interface. In this manner the actual class can be changed in the configuration file and source code would not need to be recompiled. In the following code examples some of the necessary XML syntax such as namespace declarations and container elements have been removed for clarity; please consult the product documentation for a full reference.

As mentioned above, the XML configuration file is key for wiring object dependencies together. The XML syntax is similar in Java and .NET versions with slight element name and naming convention differences; the online documentation for each is well done and it should relatively simple to translate between the environments. We will illustrate with Java Spring to be consistent with the code above. The XML configuration file to set up our basic CashRegister object is shown in Listing 7-5 and uses "setter injection" as the <property element specifies the name of the setXxx method and the name of the bean to use.

Listing 7-5. Simple XML Configuration for Spring, IoC_Config.xml

```xml
<?xml version="1.0" encoding="UTF-8"?>
<beans>
    <bean id="CashRegister" class="demo.GrocItem.CashRegister">
        <property name="priceService">
            <ref local="LookupPriceService"/>
        </property>
    </bean>
    <bean id="LookupPriceService"
            class="demo.GrocItem.LookupPriceService">
    </bean>
</beans>
```

After the configuration file is complete, the source code needs to be changed to make use of the framework. Note that once these changes are made, the source code will no longer need to be changed and recompiled when different versions of the price service are used. This insulates the code from implementation changes and allows for swapping of PriceService classes with minimal impact.

Listing 7-6. Main method using the IoC container framework

```java
public class ConsoleApp
{
    public static void main(String[] args)
    {
        ApplicationContext context =
            new ClassPathXmlApplicationContext("IoC_Config.xml");

        CashRegister cr =
                (CashRegister)context.getBean("CashRegister");

        GrocItem gi = new GrocItem("Bread");
        cr.AddItem(gi);

        // ...
    }
}
```

While these examples are admittedly simple, the principals can be easily extended to real systems. When using these principles the code will be more testable, extensible, and maintainable than code without patterns. Exploring and applying the many other patterns and frameworks available for software reuse and design will greatly enhance the quality of software being developed.

Refactoring using Patterns

Patterns are not only used when designing from the ground up - patterns are often useful targets of refactoring. As discussed in Chapter 3:, one goal of refactoring is to make code more maintainable. This aligns closely with patterns as a proper use of patterns at design-time can make an application easily extensible and more maintainable.

The two patterns used in the example will be The Factory Method Pattern and The Strategy Pattern. A brief explanation of each is given next, but for a more complete description the reader is urged to consult the previously mentioned GoF book and/or other resources that will explain these patterns and their derivatives in more detail.

Factory Method Pattern

The Factory Method pattern is used to define the creation of objects. Specifically, the Factory Method is most useful when one of many subclasses is needed but exactly which one is not determinable until run-time. This can be important in frameworks where the framework user is given the option (or sometimes required) to define custom subclasses of existing framework classes. For example, in many GUI frameworks is it common to have user applications subclass many of the framework classes; often it is even required by making the framework classes purely abstract.

A very simple example would be a `FrameworkApplication` class that uses a `FrameworkWindow` class. The `FrameworkApplication` would define a method for creating `FrameworkWindow` objects and could store, display, and manipulate them based on a known class interface. However both of these are meant to be overridden by the user of the framework. The base factory method would be overridden by the user to return the user-defined window.

A common variation of this is known as the Parameterized Factory Method. In this configuration a method in a factory class accepts a parameter and returns an object based on that parameter. The return type of the method is an interface or base class; the object returned implements the interface or is a derived class. This centralizes object creation to a known location and allows the client of the method to work with a common definition which can be expanded as necessary.

Strategy Pattern

The Strategy Pattern is used to encapsulate a specified behavior in a standard interface. Classes that implement this interface may use different algorithms or private methods to accomplish their tasks; however the outward behavior of the class should remain the same. This allows for variation in actual implementation details while the public interface is constant. Also keep in mind that thus far this pattern has been described using interfaces, but this can also be accomplished using base classes. The determination between interfaces and base classes would be if default behavior would be desired.

A common example of this would be sorting. An interface defined as ISortable with a single method Sort() would be the simple interface definition. Then several classes with more descriptive names such as BubbleSort, QSort, BucketSort, etc. would implement the interface and accomplish the Sort() behavior in their respective ways. Any code that uses the ISortable interface wouldn't need to know the implementation details, only that after calling ISortable.Sort() the user's collection is sorted.

Example

The following discussion and code is a simple example of applying patterns as a way of refactoring. It is kept over-simplified for illustrative purposes; however one could imagine it being used as a quick prototype that is then refactored to become the basis of a full system. The code in Listing 7-7 is a simple command-line procedural application that prints data in a report format: descriptive column headers and data in a columnar format. The class Report1Data is a simple container class that represents some basic data; its definition is not shown.

Although the code works, it has several shortcomings for maintainable and extensible code. Suppose additional reports were to be added and the user prompted for which report to run. Would there be additional constants for the new columns? How would the proper columns be determined? And each report could theoretically need different data sources. The short answer is that the code needs to be refactored so that these concerns are addressed – this is done by applying design patterns and making the program more object-oriented.

To address the issue of choosing and creating one of many reports, a ReportFactory class will be introduced. It will use a Parameterized Factory Method to decide which report to create and return. It will return an object that implements the IReportStrategy interface which represents a report.

Listing 7-7. Report program to be refactored using patterns

```
class Program
{
    private const string RPT_NAME = "TEST";
    private const string COL_1 = "ID";
    private const string COL_2 = "Some String";
    private const string COL_3 = "Some Number";

    static void Main(string[] args)
    {
        Console.WriteLine(RPT_NAME);
        Console.WriteLine("{0,5} {1,12} {2,12}",
                        COL_1, COL_2, COL_3);

        List<Report1Data> rptData = GetReportData();
```

```
    foreach (Report1Data item in rptData)
    {
        Console.WriteLine("{0,5} {1,12} {2,12}",
                        item.ID, item.SomeString,
                        item.SomeNumber);
    }

    Console.Write("\n\nPress Enter to quit...");
    Console.ReadLine();
}

private static List<Report1Data> GetReportData()
{
    List<Report1Data> list1 = new List<Report1Data>()
    {
        new Report1Data(){ID=1,SomeString="Jessica",
                        SomeNumber=22},
        new Report1Data(){ID=2,SomeString="Mandy",
                        SomeNumber=37},
        new Report1Data(){ID=3,SomeString="John",
                        SomeNumber=43}
    };
    return list1;
}
}
```

The code for the revised main() function is shown below. It is much cleaner than before, with knowledge of the actual report details sheltered away in the report implementation. In fact, this function could support any number of additional reports with no modification at all provided the additional reports are wired into the existing factory and strategy constructs.

Listing 7-8. Revised main function after refactoring

```
class Program
{
    static void Main(string[] args)
    {
        Console.Write("Enter the name of the report: ");
        String reportName = Console.ReadLine();

        IReportStrategy rs =
                        ReportFactory.GetReport(reportName);
        if (rs != null)
```

```
    {
        Console.WriteLine(rs.GetColumnHeaders());

        for (int i = 0; i < rs.GetNumberOfRows(); i++)
            Console.WriteLine(rs.GetData(i));
    }
    else
        Console.WriteLine("Report {0} not found.",
                            reportName);

        Console.Write("\n\nPress Enter to quit...");
        Console.ReadLine();
    }
}
```

The definition of the ReportFactory and IReportStategy are shown on the next page. Both of these are fairly simple and self-explanatory in this example. Note that the factory method is the only entity that has to know about all the reports. This is the code proof of the statement earlier concerning centralized object creation.

Listing 7-9. Simple Strategy Inteface

```
interface IReportStrategy
{
    String GetReportName();
    String GetColumnHeaders();
    int GetNumberOfRows();
    String GetData(int nRow);
}
```

Listing 7-10. Simple factory method class

```
class ReportFactory
{
    public static IReportStrategy GetReport(String rptName)
    {
        IReportStrategy strat = null;
        if (rptName.Equals("Report1"))
            strat = new Report1();
        else if (rptName.Equals("Report2"))
            strat = new Report2();

        return strat;
    }
}
```

Finally, what does an implementation class look like? Each report knows about its own columns and can load its own data. Notice that in this implementation the LoadData() function is called in the constructor, but another viable alternative would be to have the LoadData() function be public and called only be the client. This is purely a design decision and doesn't affect the application of the pattern.

Listing 7-11. Strategy Implementation Class

```
class Report1 : IReportStrategy
{
    List<Report1Data> _data = new List<Report1Data>();

    public Report1() { LoadData(); }

    public string GetReportName() { return "Test Report"; }

    public string GetColumnHeaders()
    {
        return String.Format("{0,5} {1,12} {2,12}",
                    "ID", "SomeString", "SomeNumber");
    }

    public int GetNumberOfRows() { return _data.Count; }

    public string GetData(int nRow)
    {
        Report1Data rd = _data[nRow];
        return String.Format("{0,5} {1,12} {2,12}",
                    rd.ID, rd.SomeString, rd.SomeNumber);
    }

    private void LoadData()
    {
        _data.AddRange(new List<Report1Data>()
        {
        new Report1Data(){ID=1, SomeString="Jessica",
                            SomeNumber=22},
        new Report1Data(){ID=2, SomeString="Mandy",
                            SomeNumber=37},
        new Report1Data(){ID=3, SomeString="John",
                            SomeNumber=43}
        });
    }
}
```

As shown the interface and implementing methods use basic string objects instead of actual data-centric constructs such as `DataRow`, `DataColumn`, or `DataTable`. Also, the "data" is simply a list of made-up data objects. This is a function of the simplistic console example; real implementations would typically expose more complex return types and pull data from a database, web service, or other legitimate data source. That would allow other clients, such as desktop applications and web clients to use the factory as well. Any class that implemented the interface would be usable as a report.

Other than actual data framework objects, how could it be improved? Other possible improvements would be for the `ReportFactory` to return a list of valid report names to be used by the client (for use in a drop-down list box for graphical clients), the total number of reports, or other factory metadata.

Architecture Pattern: N-Tier

While the patterns discussed in the previous sections dealt with software architecture, this section moves toward hardware architecture as it applies to software design. The intent is not to fully discuss the details at the infrastructure and/or network engineer level but rather to give a brief understanding of how hardware architecture can affect software design and implementation.

While sometimes referred to as "3-tier" a more accurate description would be "N-tier" where "N" is a number greater-than or equal to three. "3-tier" was the name originally given as the natural progression from strict client-server (2-tier) architecture, but over time even more processing layers have been introduced to promote extensibility and resiliency as systems have become more complex. In addition, an application that has three conceptual (logical) tiers may have a different number of physical tiers; this will be further discussed in the following paragraphs.

Figure 7-5 depicts the classic 3-tier architecture scheme. While similar to the MVC software pattern in that each component is responsible for a specific operation, each component in a 3-tier architecture is a logical layer representing at least one physical component and possibly more. This is also affected by choices in communication medium between the layers – normal network protocols wouldn't necessarily introduce more layers but using message queues or some other type of guaranteed delivery service between components would produce additional layers.

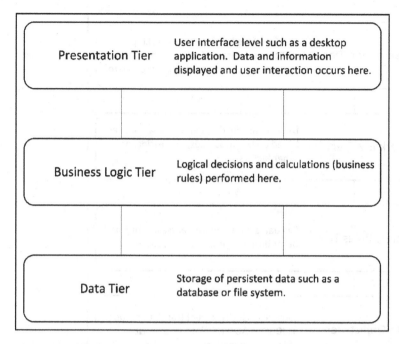

Figure 7-5. *Classic 3-tier architecture*

Another popular way of adding more layers is using technology available in each layer to enforce redundant security and business rules. Using database stored procedures in the data tier to double-check business rules would introduce another layer to the application but would provide additional security such as against hackers that may attempt to bypass those checks in the application at a higher level. Likewise, splitting the business logic layer into a workflow layer and a business rules layer is common, as workflow products have become increasingly popular. The workflow layer controls which screens the user sees and what they are allowed to do; the business rules layer evaluates data and enforces business rules in a data-centric fashion.

Figure 7-6 shows a diagram of a multiple-tier architecture with the additional tiers in place. While possibly introducing some complexity due to these additional layers, each layer can also be insulated from changes in the other layers through proper use of interfaces and software design patterns discussed earlier.

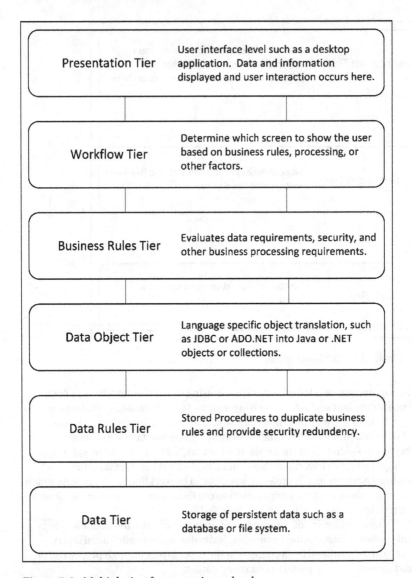

Presentation Tier	User interface level such as a desktop application. Data and information displayed and user interaction occurs here.
Workflow Tier	Determine which screen to show the user based on business rules, processing, or other factors.
Business Rules Tier	Evaluates data requirements, security, and other business processing requirements.
Data Object Tier	Language specific object translation, such as JDBC or ADO.NET into Java or .NET objects or collections.
Data Rules Tier	Stored Procedures to duplicate business rules and provide security redundency.
Data Tier	Storage of persistent data such as a database or file system.

Figure 7-6. *Multiple tiers for processing redundancy*

So what does each of these look like in the real world? Keep in mind the diagrams in Figure 7-5 and Figure 7-6 are logical diagrams. With actual implementation some of the layers may reside on the same server, while sometimes a "tier" may be split across multiple physical servers. It may depend on the software being used, the rules mandated by corporate policy, or any number of factors.

For example, it is common for the web server and application server to be combined on one physical machine. Sometimes the application server isn't even present as a separate entity; business logic is compiled into separate modules (dlls or library files) and loaded from within the web processing logic.

A simple physical diagram is shown below in Figure 7-7. Notice how the web server and component libraries are co-located, thus combining the presentation layer and business logic layer onto a single server. In this case the firewall can also be thought of as part of the business logic as it can be programmed to deny connections from certain locations.

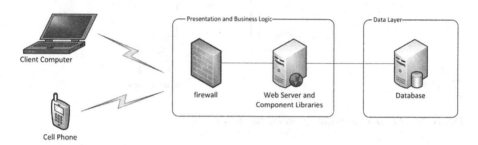

Figure 7-7. *Example 3-tier physical architecture*

An example of this from the software world would be a Microsoft ASP.NET application using classes that are compiled into separate DLL assemblies and loaded when needed. In a Java web application this could be a servlet class rendering the display but also accessing business logic JARs residing somewhere else on the server. Although it is not depicted directly on the diagram, only the business logic should access the database directly. The presentation layer talks only to the business layer; the business layer communicates with both the presentation layer and the data layer.

There is one final note about the data and business layers in Figure 7-7. As it is shown the business logic appears to be contained completely on the web server. This is in keeping with our previous discussion regarding DLLs or jar files. However, the business logic could be programmed entirely in stored procedures. In this case the business logic layer would reside on the database and it would then have the combined title of "Business Logic and Data Layer".

Complexity of the application, the number of outside systems requiring an interface, and plain old corporate policy may also dictate the physical architecture of an application. The application shown below in Figure 7-8 has several features of a typical enterprise application. In this case, the diagram also has the same logical components described in Figure 7-6. The layers may overlap significantly and contain multiple servers, so rather than showing the layers on the diagram first, the purpose for each piece of the application will be explained and the layers will be described verbally.

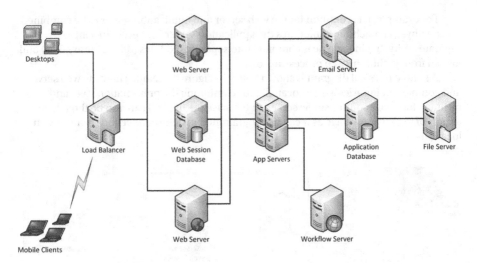

Figure 7-8. *Complex application, multi-tier architecture*

First the web servers. Corporate policy for this imaginary application states that the application must be available all the time, even during maintenance, and that it must have a resilient design. To implement this, a load-balancing server (LBS) is used and will decide which web server to access. If one server is down or too busy, incoming traffic will automatically be directed to the other server. This arrangement requires the web session data, which is normally stored in memory, to be stored in a database. This is because if a user has multiple requests that use session data and those requests are handled by different servers, the session data must be available. So from a logical standpoint the LBS, two web servers, and session database are the presentation layer.

The App Servers contain multiple logical components. The business rules tier and the data object tier are both present on these servers. Not only do the app servers use programming logic to enforce business rules, they may also consult with the workflow tier (a separate server in this diagram) for certain operational decisions. Data objects would be used in this layer to send to the presentation layer for display and to the workflow server for processing and/or evaluation. The app servers also use a separate email server for sending outgoing notification; hence it shown separately in the diagram. As the email server may be asked to send out email in response to certain conditions it could be thought of as part of the business rules tier.

The application database also has two logical components on it; the data rules tier and the data tier. The data rules tier exists as stored procedures, constraints, and database functions that duplicate and/or extend the business tier that exists on the app server.

The data tier actually could include the file server as well. The database doesn't store data locally; instead it uses a file server to provide file space that is separate from the database server. This is typically done in large enterprise applications for resiliency and ease of adding new space.

The diagram including the logical tiers is shown in Figure 7-9. Please note that there could be many ways to do this. For example, some would argue that the email server is a separate system altogether and should be included as a part of the data objects and not the business rules. Or that the web session database is actually part of the data tier. The point however, is NOT to ensure that all logical to physical mapping is absolutely correct; there are no concrete standards for this. The intent is to demonstrate some general guidelines and then be able to use those guidelines for ensuring that all logical tiers have a mapping to *somewhere* and are all accounted for. Keeping the logical to physical mapping is sync can also be useful to determine the impact of upgrades, patches, and ensuring that all servers are being used. If the workflow application was removed and implemented entirely in program logic, the architecture diagram allow determination of which servers to be removed.

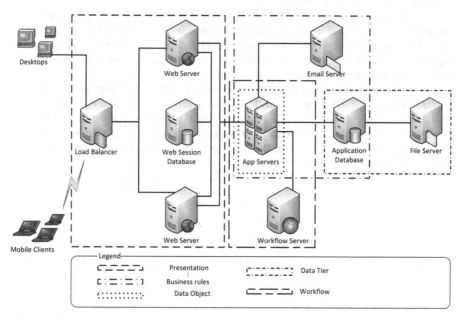

Figure 7-9. *Complex application with logical tiers*

One final note relating to enterprise architecture: depending on the complexity of the system, size of the organization, corporate policy, and regulatory statutes, the system pictured in Figure 7-9 could have sister environments for development, user-testing, and especially disaster recovery. This means that each of the servers shown could have three (or more) counterparts performing the same job but used at different times in the life cycle of the application. Architecture diagrams assist in keeping all of the organized and ensure the different environments are roughly the same.

Summary

Patterns, both software and architecture, are important to understand and be able to apply. Understanding software patterns not only allows the construction of better code, but also allows for better usage of pre-existing code if that code is documented as being part of a particular pattern. Testing and extensibility are also important reasons to use patterns in distributed systems, especially when implementing multi-tier architecture where other components may be implemented by other teams. These remote components may not be available for testing and patterns such as the Inversion of Control allow for testing with mock objects.

Patterns are also commonly used in refactoring. Simplistic prototype programs may need to be refactored into production-capable code. Existing code may need to be expanded or re-written from its current state. Using patterns as a target of refactoring will improve the maintainability and extensibility of the original code, as well as potentially preserve much of the work already in place.

An application can be represented by both logical and physical diagrams. Clear separation on one type does not mean clear separation on the other. For example, business logic is often combined on the same server as presentation logic. Conversely, business rules may be split between and/or duplicated on both the application server and the database server. Complexity, outside interfaces, and corporate policy may be factors in dictating the architecture of a system.

■ ■ ■

CHAPTER 8

Software Requirements

Writing good requirements is difficult. Interpreting bad requirements is even tougher. In this section we will define requirements from a couple of different perspectives, discuss how the different perspectives work together, and list some general recommendations about each. We will also cover the roles the developers play in the requirements process and why developing and interpreting requirements are important skills. As with many of the topics in this book, there are countless permutations of the concepts we are trying to cover and other works that are dedicated solely to the topic of requirements. Here we present a general overview with an emphasis on aspects that are important to developers from an enterprise or large organization perspective.

In our previous sections on Test Driven Development and the Agile method we discussed minimal documentation and using index cards or story cards to capture desired behavior. Here we address the other extreme – documenting requirements in a more traditional way so that both the business and technical project managers can track their status through the life of a project. In this chapter we will use a human resources time-card application as our target system. All examples will be in the context of developing this as an internal application for internal users. Similar concepts apply to external and retail applications however.

Business Requirements

Business analysts – those familiar with the day-to-day operations of the end users – will usually be instrumental in bridging the gap between business terminology and technical implementation. These analysts will assist in documenting requirements (described later) and will represent the business users to the technical staff in discussions.

At the highest level of abstraction is the Vision Statement, sometimes referred to as Primary Business Goal. This is a document or statement usually written from the business perspective describing the overall strategic goal of the software. Typically this statement is brief; only a few sentences or paragraphs long. One theoretical goal statement is shown below in Figure 8-1.

> To provide employees and management with an easy-to-use electronic time-card system that allows tracking of work, vacation, holidays, volunteer time, and other work related activities.

Figure 8-1. *Time card application Vision Statement*

The statement is admittedly simple and brief, but the high-level purpose of the system is summed up in a single statement.

The vision statement describes the overall purpose of the application and may not necessarily need to be changed with each additional feature. However, for major changes (or when starting from scratch) the first document constructed is typically a Business Requirements Document, often referred to as a BRD. In this document the business, with the assistance of the business analyst, spells out in business terms what the software should do. The document is typically written in business terms; the technical team will create their own document spelling out the technical details needed to accomplish what the business wants.

Use cases are another higher-level abstraction that begins to show interaction with the system. Actors are defined and are shown interacting with specific processes or components that produce a specific outcome. It is a standard convention that a use case begins with a verb before the component being acted upon (Wiegers, 2006). There are several ways to define use cases; the two most common being a use case diagram in UML and a more detailed written description.

In Figure 8-2 an overly simplified use case diagram for some of the operations in the example time card system is shown. In this diagram there are four actors and six use cases; this shows that use cases may be shared among actors. Also note that each use case is a meaningful action that is carried out by each actor. The diagram doesn't show any restrictions or special conditions. When more detail is needed for a use case the diagram is supplemented with a written description.

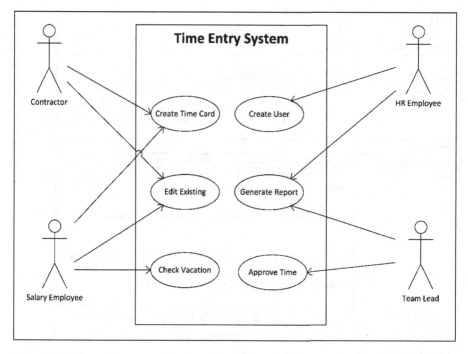

Figure 8-2. *Example use-case diagram*

Formatting for the written description varies widely and the example presented here is one of many formats. The amount of information and level of detail can differ depending on the complexity of the use case, the use of standard templates, or other organizational and/or team factors. Sometimes a use case can be an informal paragraph, but the example we show here is moderately more complex. In the example HR timecard system each use case in the diagram would be matched by a corresponding use case description. The example shown in Figure 8-3 is loosely based on the template in (Wiegers, 2006) but as mentioned above, many formats are available and there is no single industry standard use case description template.

Use Case Name:	Create Time Card
Created by:	EC
Date Created:	8-1-2011
Actors:	Contractor, Salaried Employee
Description:	Actors should be able to create a time card for a specific reporting period. They should be able to add tasks and hours for those tasks for the period and mark it "ready for review" when done.
Priority:	1
Assumptions:	Actors set up with proper projects and task choices.
Rules:	Actors can save a time card without completing it – they may enter the entire period at once or update daily. Before marking "ready for review" each day must have an entry. Two time cards cannot be created for the same payroll period. Contractors are not allowed to enter vacation time.
Preconditions:	Actors successfully sign onto the system.
Notes:	

Figure 8-3. *Example Use Case written description*

In addition to or sometimes in place of use cases, the BRD may include more specific business user requirements spelled out in sentence form. These items may map more closely to the technical implementation. In fact they may actually spell out some specific items to be implemented in the source code. In the above written description the "Rules" section most closely resembles these specific requirements but in a typical BRD these "line items" have identifiers that project managers and team leads can use to address a specific item. The table below in Figure 8-4 shows a small sample of this type of BRD entry.

ID:	Description	Priority	Status
R-11	Users should not have to sign into the system; their current network login should be used for identification.	Med	Done
R-12	The user should pick a project first; the tasks available are a derivative of the project.	High	Open
R-13	A full-time employee should not be able to submit a time card with less than 40 hours per week recorded.	High	Open
R-14	A contractor can submit any number of hours up to 60 without special approval	Med	Open
R-15	A team lead can see his/her team's time cards before they are submitted but cannot approve them until the user submits it.	High	Open
R-16	Each approver should have a surrogate approver with the same approval rights.	High	Open
R-17	If the user attempts to submit a time card without an entry for each day, the user should see an alert stating "Time card incomplete" and the action should fail.	High	Open
R-18	If a user is inactive for 5 minutes the system will timeout and kick the user off	Low	Open

Figure 8-4. Example User Requirements

Note that the sample above is an overly simple example and most likely a real BRD would have additional columns. These might be a requirement category, such as "System", "Legal", "Performance", etc. There could also be a "Notes" column for additional information, a "Date" for when the requirement was added, a desired release number if the project is in phases, and more. The main point is that the above statements are from the business perspective and while not technical, care must be taken to understand exactly how a business expectation translates into a technical implementation. For example, a business requirement of "User should be able to search entire intranet for search term in less than one second" is likely unattainable and that sort of requirement should be tempered in consultation with the business analyst.

Functional Design

Once the business requirements have been completed, another typical piece of documentation is the Function System Design, or FSD. In many organizations this serves two purposes: to address the coverage of the business requirements and to specify the actual system implementation down to the class, object, and possibly even the sequence diagram level. In other scenarios it simply focuses as a logical design document to ensure that all aspects of the Business Requirements are covered. As there are plenty of other references on classes, objects, object-oriented design and sequence diagrams, here we will address the coverage of the business requirements. Later on we will discuss technical specifications at a high level in a section on Technical Design.

As stated for the other items in this section, there are countless formats, templates, and structured documents that may be called an FSD. The focus in this section is to show a mapping between the requirements in Figure 8-4 and a functional statement that implements the requirement in question. Often times this is referred to as a "traceability matrix" and can provide a way of verifying that all requirements are covered by at least one functional design statement.

One representation involves the creation of a set of statements similar to Figure 8-4; however, these statements describe technical aspects of the system. They would also have an additional column stating which requirement in the BRD is covered by this functional statement. These two columns could easily be extracted into a matrix to compare the mappings between business requirement ID and function requirement ID.

ID:	Description	Bus Req	Status
F-23	The system will use Windows integrated authentication for identifying the user.	R-11	Assigned
F-24	The list of active tasks will not be retrieved until a project is selected. These will be child-parent tables in the database and can be associated easily.	R-12	Open
F-25	The session timeout will be configurable and default to 5 minutes.	R-18	Assigned

Figure 8-5. *Sample FSD statement showing requirement number*

Another popular format is to lift the requirements table from the BRD and insert it directly into the functional design. An additional column is then added to the table which shows the functional implementation directly alongside the requirement. This is shown in Figure 8-6.

ID:	BRD Description	Functional Solution
R-11 F-23	Uses should not have to sign into the system; their current network login should be used for identification.	The system will use Windows integrated authentication for identifying the user.
R-18 F-25	If a user is inactive for 5 minutes the system will timeout and kick the user off	The session timeout will be configurable and default to 5 minutes.

Figure 8-6. *Combined FSD and BRD*

Technical Design

While the BRD and FSD are generally written at a high level so that both analysts and developers can interpret the information, "technical design" is a term given to documentation that is targeted toward developers. While some teams may have a standard "Technical Design Document (TDD)" or "Software Design Document (SDD)", multiple documents can also make up the technical design documentation. The most basic of these would be the flowchart, but others are common as well. These could include:

- Database design diagram

- UML diagrams, such as class diagram, sequence diagram, etc.

- API documentation

- Architecture diagrams

An introduction to database design is discussed in Chapter 9: Just Enough SQL and a basic database diagram is shown in Figure 9-1. In short, the database diagram shows the structure of the database such as the table names and data types, constraints, and relationships. Refer to Chapter 9 for more information.

UML (Unified Modeling Language) is a way to express several aspects of a software project. A use-case diagram has already been shown in Figure 8-2; this section will discuss lower-level diagrams such as the class diagram and sequence diagram. There are many more possible diagrams and covering them all is beyond the scope of this book. The reader should refer to Appendix D for additional resources.

A class diagram is a representation of the static class structure of an application. It illustrates class names, attributes, operations, and relationships between classes. The following two figures show the beginnings of a class diagram for the time tracker application discussed in this section.

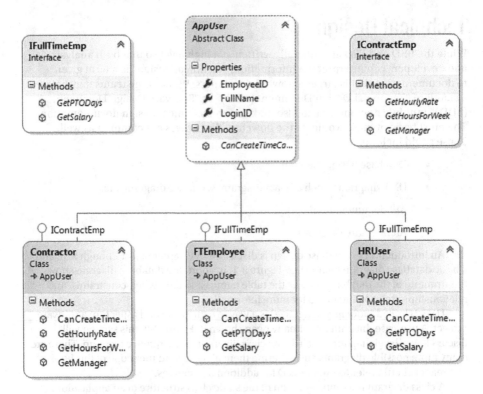

Figure 8-7. *Very simple class diagram*

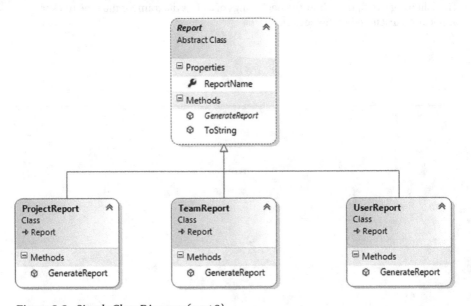

Figure 8-8. *Simple Class Diagram (part 2)*

Obviously these are very early-on diagrams; as the application progresses the diagrams may become much more complex. Keep in mind also that there are several different ways of generating these diagrams. Some development tools will automatically create diagrams based on the project structure, but diagrams are often done beforehand and maintained manually by using tools such as Microsoft Visio®.

Sequence diagrams represent the internal moving pieces of software. These diagrams illustrate what is going on at the object and method level. They highlight method calls, method return values, and object lifetimes. An example is shown in Figure 8-9 on the next page.

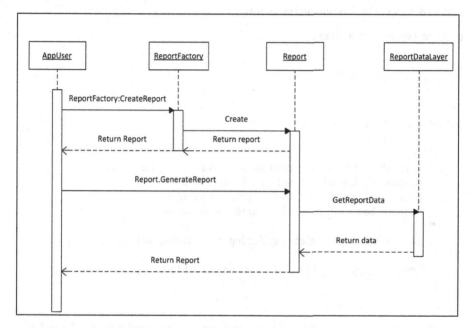

Figure 8-9. *Sequence Diagram*

There are generally two levels of detail for sequence diagrams. Some are at a somewhat higher level and don't specify actual method names or parameters, only actions and interactions. These are useful for reviewing object interactions and getting a sense for how many objects are needed to produce a desired result. Other sequence diagrams can be very detailed, specifying actual method names with parameters, looping structures, and more.

API documentation is among the very lowest level of technical documentation. Simply put, every method of every class, its parameters and return value, and sometimes even usage context is included in this documentation. Numerous examples of this exist online, the most prevalent being Microsoft's MSDN documentation for the .NET library and Oracle's JavaDoc documentation.

As with class diagrams, this information can be generated manually or automatically. Manual creation of this documentation is done using a simple text editor. However a more popular way of creating this type of documentation is through documentation comments in the source code itself. These are specially formatted comments with specific keywords. These are very similar to normal comments except for the special identifiers and tags. Tools exist for taking these comments and producing standard format documentation in various formats such as html or XML.

The following figure shows an example of the comment format in Java that is used to produce the documentation.

Listing 8-1. Java documentation comments

```java
package com.nokelservices;

/**
 * @author Author Name
 *
 */
public class SettingValidator
{
    /**
     * Validates the given key/value pair for allowable values
     * @param key key of the setting to validate
     * @param value value of the setting to validate
     * @return boolean indicating valid value or not
     */
    public boolean isValidSetting(String key, String value)
    {
        return (key.length() > 0 && value.length() > 0);
    }
}
```

These comments can be applied to the package, class and methods, as well as other types such as structures and enumerations. There are also more tags than are shown here, please refer to the online documentation for a complete list and their uses. Once these comments are processed a web-based application is built that follows a standard format. Figure 8-10 is the page generated from the above Java code and comments.

com.nokelservices
Class SettingValidator

```
java.lang.Object
  └ com.nokelservices.SettingValidator
```

```
public class SettingValidator
extends java.lang.Object
```

Author:
> Author Name

Constructor Summary

```
SettingValidator()
```

Method Summary

boolean	`isValidSetting`(java.lang.String key, java.lang.String value)
	Validates the given key/value pair for allowable values

Methods inherited from class java.lang.Object

```
equals, getClass, hashCode, notify, notifyAll, toString, wait, wait, wait
```

Constructor Detail

SettingValidator

```
public SettingValidator()
```

Method Detail

isValidSetting

```
public boolean isValidSetting(java.lang.String key,
                              java.lang.String value)
```

> Validates the given key/value pair for allowable values

> **Parameters:**
>> key - key of the setting to validate
>> value - value of the setting to validate
> **Returns:**
>> boolean indicating valid value or not

Package **Class** Use Tree Deprecated Index Help

PREV CLASS   NEXT CLASS
SUMMARY: NESTED | FIELD | CONSTR | METHOD

FRAMES   NO FRAMES
DETAIL: FIELD | CONSTR | METHOD

Figure 8-10. Sample JavaDoc page

Other languages may have their own commenting standards and procedures for documenting code. As stated above, the .NET version of documentation comments is very similar to the preceding Java format. PHP and Perl also have standards for creating code from comments.

The architecture diagram is highlighted in Chapter 7 as part of the pattern discussion. These diagrams are also often included in technical documentation. Not only are they useful for "big picture" discussions but they are also useful in determining which teams to partner with and how many other teams will be necessary. Also, special hardware situations such as clustering and firewalls may be depicted in these diagrams, which may or may not result in some special code considerations.

Change Control

In the discussion of Agile software frequent release cycles led to the requirements being updated and reprioritized often. In a system where rigid documentation principles are followed that is typically not allowed to happen. Rather, after the requirements and design documents are completed and approved, any changes in requirements or the design implementation must follow a formal change control process. This is not to prevent changes to the system, but rather to properly analyze and document them (Weigers, 2003). This also helps to limit "scope creep" which is where many small changes accumulate to become a major change to the system implementation. If these aren't properly vetted and documented they will cause the project to be late or improperly implemented. Through this process some may be implemented right away; some may be designated as a requirement in a future release of the product.

Again, there are countless policies for handling change control as well as countless ways of documenting the process. Some organizations may use an email trail, some may use a "mini-BRD/FSD" structure, and still others may blend the two based on the severity of the change. Ideally all changes should follow the same system and the discussion in this section only outlines a single change control process. Also, we only briefly discuss the surrounding process and focus mainly on the documentation of the change.

In the time card project let us assume that the BRD is complete and approved, the FSD is complete and approved, and actual coding has begun. After reviewing the document and current practices in a legacy system, the business analyst comes to the development team and states that there was a scenario that was missed and could slightly change the flow.

The new requirement is this: "a team lead may need to complete and approve a time card on behalf of the team members". This leads to the creation of a change request (CR) that will formally document this new requirement as part of the change control process.

For clarity and tracking purposes, each change request should be documented in a single document. Like requirements a CR is given a unique identifier and has a brief description. However, because it is arriving after the design is complete and the coding has started, many more questions and factors have to be considered before adopting the new requirement as part of the implementation. Again, documentation standards vary widely, but a sample CR with additional questions and sample answers appears in Figure 8-11.

ID:	CR-100
Issue:	New Requirement
Description:	A team lead may need to complete and approve a time card on behalf of the team members. This could happen in rare situations where a person is sick the day timecards need submitted, the person is on vacation when timecards are due, or the person is unable to connect to the system when cards are due.
Original Req ID:	N/A
Priority:	High
Users affected?	Yes
Use Case ID:	"Approve Time"
Stage Discovered:	Development
Discovered By:	Business Analyst
Test Case ID:	N/A
Retest Required?	No
Database change?	No
Business rule change?	Yes
User interface change?	Yes (minor only to team lead)
Development Impact:	Current business rules will have to change to allow for a team lead to complete and submit a time card on behalf of a team member. The time card will have to be annotated to this fact and the user should receive notification that this occurred.
Work around?	No work around exists – if not implemented time cards could be late and employee pay may be affected.

Figure 8-11. Sample CR documentation

The additional questions and documentation on a CR help to determine whether to include the item as part of the current release or move it to later release. Some organizations use a Change Control Board (CCB) to review all CRs and determine where and when they will be implemented. The CCB typically consists of project managers, development team leads and/or managers, and occasionally a business partner. Each has a different area of interest and will examine the CR for their concerns. The development manager's concern centers on topics such as additional coding, change to current code, and the time required. The business partner's concerns are around user effectiveness (do they need this new functionality right now or is there a work-around?) and release date impact. And the project manager is typically concerned with impact to both the release schedule and budget. As a CR is spread among these many concerns, the additional documentation and process is usually justified.

Summary

Requirements and design documentation play an important role in the software development process. Requirements detail what is desired to get accomplished; functional designs describe how it will be done. Although there are many different formats and techniques the overall goals are the same. Being able to interpret and evaluate the desires of the business partner or customer will help not only to achieve what is desired, but not to over commit to unrealistic expectations.

In many organizations this documentation process is still followed although the coding of the system may use other techniques, such as Agile development, to actually produce the software. BRDs and FSDs are used and tracked by project managers while the implementation is managed by the development team. The development team may use various pieces of technical documentation to describe the details of the software. This low-level technical documentation may not be reviewed by anyone outside the development team, or parts of it may be used for communication with other teams such as infrastructure or testing. As long as the implementation process produces the product in line with the project manager's delivery schedule everyone is happy.

■ ■ ■

CHAPTER 9

Just Enough SQL

Structured Query Language (SQL) was once thought of just for database administrators (DBAs) or dedicated database developers. In many organizations however, the DBA's main purpose is support of production systems, and database development is left to the application team.

As mentioned below in Appendix A, a large organization will typically have separate regions for development, user testing, and production. The limitations of this arrangement are discussed further in the appendix, but in this section we assume the situation exists where the application developer also has the ability to both create and directly query the database for data. This is a fairly typical arrangement, as the finished development database will then be re-created in the higher testing and production environments. At this time the DBAs may take look and offer suggestions or discuss limitations based on corporate database policy, but often times the development environment is left open and the application team is expected to fully create and program the database objects for the application.

In addition, application teams may be given read-only access in higher environments. This would be done to assist in trouble-shooting application errors. For instance, in a test or production environment, if an application is behaving strangely and the logs do not show logic errors, the suspicion may be the problem is data related. In this case an application developer may need to inspect the data directly using SQL statements.

Given the above statements, this section will discuss the following topics:

- Minimal database design

- Basic SQL statements for operating with data

- More advanced SQL – joins and sub-queries

- Programming libraries and frameworks for interacting with a database

- Advanced programming frameworks such as object-relational mapping (ORM) tools.

A Note about the Server and Client Tools

Normally, database servers are separate machines – servers locked away somewhere that only the DBAs have direct and unlimited access to, even for development servers. As is the case for many examples in this book, the environment is being simplified by using a local database server. While there are several free products to choose from, many with retail production equivalents (Oracle Express and Oracle, SQL Express and SQL Server), this section will use both the free MySQL server and corresponding GUI client tool (available at www.mysql.com/downloads at the time of this writing) and SQL Server Express and the corresponding Management Studio. The concepts of design and syntax for querying are similar to the other products, while both the database engines and GUI clients are lightweight and easy to install. Any concepts and principals discussed and shown here can easily be transferred to other database environments. Links to the SQL scripts to recreate the database will be given at the end of the chapter.

Minimal Database Design

Although there are many types of storage available, the vast majority of applications store their data in a relational database. "Relational" in the sense that many domain objects are contained within a database and related to each other through database constructs. The database that will be discussed here is called "StoreInventory" (StoreInventoryDB in MS SQL) and represents the information for a typical retail store software application. As with the rest of the examples in the book, the database will be extremely simplified to discuss the important concepts rather than creating a fully implemented production quality database. The concepts discussed here can be scaled to include a more complex system.

The simplified example system, shown in Figure 9-1, is represented in a typical Entity Relationship (ER) diagram. The name of each table, its columns, each column type, and the relationships between the tables is shown. Without completely restating database design theory, the following are important notes about this database:

- The database has three primary objects – Store, Product, and Category. Each entity maintains information only about itself; this is referred to a normalizing the database.

- Category and Product have a one-to-many relationship through the foreign key field of "CategoryID" in the Product table relating to "idCatgory" primary key in the Category table. That is, a Category can describe many Products, but a Product can only have one Category.

- Product and Store have a many-to-many relationship, shown by using a junction table named "Store_Product". This means that a Product can be in multiple stores, and a Store can have multiple products.

- The junction table also has a "Quantity" column to keep track of the number of products in a store. In a more complicated design this may be in a separate table, such as "Inventory", but in this simple example it will be in the junction table.

- The "LocationType" column in Store should only be "U", "S", or "R" representing Urban, Suburban, and Rural respectively. Many databases support this type of data restriction with a "Check Constraint"; however MySQL doesn't support this type of constraint. We mention it simply as an example that may be seen in other database systems and won't discuss check constraints at length.

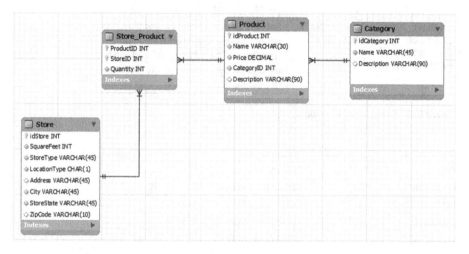

Figure 9-1. *Simple database system*

SQL Statement Basics

The downloadable SQL scripts (more details in Appendix C.) illustrate both the database object creation statements and repetitive `insert` statements used to seed the database. Although it is important to understand them from a syntax point-of-view, here we work from the standpoint that the database and data already exist. The statements discussed would be useful for data verification or troubleshooting.

The most basic of all SQL statements is the `select` statement; it has the basic form shown below. Note that even though in general SQL is NOT case sensitive, SQL keywords will be shown in all caps to differentiate them from database objects.

Listing 9-1. Form of the basic select statement

```
SELECT columnlist FROM table
```

Although extremely simple, this format is the building block for all statements to come. The `columnlist` signifies a list of named columns or calculated values to retrieve from the `table` object, which in actuality can be a table, view, or some another statement. The following table shows and explains some basic examples.

`SELECT * FROM product`	Uses the shortcut "*" syntax; returns all columns from the product table.

`SELECT Name`
`, Price`
`, Description`
`FROM product`
	Only return the Name, Price, and Description columns (note this style of putting ", " at the start of a line allows for easily adding and removing columns with comments)

`SELECT Name as ItemName`
`, Price as ItemPrice`
`, Description`
`FROM product`
	Same results as above except that in the results will show as ItemName and ItemPrice. This is "aliasing" and can be used to present user-friendly column header names.

Figure 9-2. *Sample Select Statements*

Product Name	Item Price	Item Description	Category Number
Battery	100	Standard car battery	1
Head Lamps	25	Replacment head lamps	1
Oil Filter	6	Replacment oil filter	1
Lug Wrench	12	Wrench for changing tires	1
Car Jack	75	3-ton jack for small cars	1
Air Freshener	2	Mirror mounted scent wafer	1
Vent Air Freshener	3	Freshener that mounts in air vent	1
4GB USB Thumb drive	8	USB Digital Media, removable, 4GB	2
8GB USB Thumb drive	14	USB Digital Media, removable, 8GB	2
42 inch LCD TV	600	Flat Screen TV, 42 inch picture	2
52 inch LCD TV	900	Flat Screen TV, 52 inch picture	2

Figure 9-3. *Partial Result*

The above result set shows the partial result of a simple select statement. As an exercise, write the statement that would produce it (answer in the appendix).

Filtering and Sorting

The select statements in the previous section are the bare minimum for retrieving data from a database table. Usually the data will need to be filtered and/or ordered when viewing. So rather than seeing all Products in whatever order the database returns them in, Products may need to be seen in alphabetical order; or only items with the phrase

'USB' in them; or only in a specific category. The following expanded select statement shows the additional clauses used for performing these actions:

Listing 9-2. Filtering and Ordering

```
SELECT columnlist FROM table
WHERE columnCondition
ORDER BY columnOrder (ASC|DESC)
```

The `columnCondition` clause uses comparison operators against the specified column or columns to include only rows that match the condition. The standard comparison operators, (<, <=, >, >=, !=, <>) can be used, as well as some range and set predicates such as `BETWEEN()` and `IN()`. The comparator `IS (NOT) NULL` checks to see if a null value is (not) present. Note also that multiple individual expressions may be combined with the logical operators `OR` and `AND` to evaluate the overall matching condition.

`SELECT Name, Price FROM product WHERE Price = 100.00`	Returns the Name and Price of all items whose Price is exactly 100.00.
`SELECT Name, Price FROM product WHERE CategoryID = 2`	Returns the Name and Price of all items in Category 2.
`SELECT Name, Price FROM product WHERE Price < 25`	Returns the Name and Price of all items with a Price less than 25
`SELECT Name, Price FROM product WHERE CategoryID IN (1, 2, 4)`	Returns all products with a CategoryID of 1, 2, or 4.
`SELECT Name, Price FROM product WHERE Price BETWEEN 50 AND 100`	Returns all products with a price between 50 and 100 using the BETWEEN predicate
`SELECT Name, Price FROM product WHERE Price >= 50 AND Price <= 100`	Equivalent to the above query using standard comparators ANDed together.
`SELECT Name, Price FROM product WHERE Price < 25 AND CategoryID IN (1,2)`	Returns all products from category 1 and 2 with a Price less than 25.

Figure 9-4. *Example comparison statements (numeric)*

For comparing strings there are two types of matches – exact and non-exact. The exact matching uses the "=" operator for comparison to a given string value; all strings in ISO SQL are enclosed in single quotes. The non-exact operator uses the LIKE() predicate and wild-card specifiers _ and % to signify one and many characters respectively. Examples of these expressions are shown below in Figure 9-5. Note that some databases may have support for more advanced regular expressions but those won't be discussed here as regular expressions are a topic all by themself.

SELECT * FROM Product WHERE Name = 'Battery'	Returns all products with the exact name of "Battery".
SELECT * FROM Product WHERE Name LIKE 'Drive%'	Returns all products that start with the phrase "Drive".
SELECT * FROM Product WHERE Name = '%USB%'	Returns all products that have the term "USB" somewhere in the Name.
SELECT * FROM Product WHERE Name = 'L_g%'	Returns all products that start with "Log", "Lug", etc. Any character between the L and g is valid.
SELECT * FROM Product WHERE Name NOT LIKE 'Patio%'	Returns all products that do not begin with "Patio"
SELECT * FROM Product WHERE Name IN ('Battery', 'Cup Set', 'Stapler')	Returns products that have the name of "Battery", "Cup Set", or "Stapler". Note only exact matches are possible with the IN() predicate.
SELECT * FROM Product WHERE Name LIKE 'Drive%' OR Name LIKE '%USB%'	Returns all products that begin with "Drive" or have "USB" in the name.

Figure 9-5. Example comparison statements (string)

Note that with string comparison, case may or may not be important; that is usually set as a property of the database. If needed, most databases have UPPER() and LOWER() functions that will ensure all upper- or lower-case comparisons, such as WHERE UPPER(Name) LIKE UPPER('%Usb%'). Also, spaces at the end of a string may falsify an exact match unexpectedly. Using the TRIM() function removes spaces at both ends of a string.

Thus far the order in which the recordsets are returned has not been specified. When looking at Figure 9-3 it might seem that the records are returned in order of CategoryID, but that is not the case. In fact they are returned in the order of the primary key of the table being queried; in this case ProductID. In examining the SQL used to generate the Product table it would be seen that the order shown in Figure 9-3 is indeed the order in which the items were inserted into the table.

As shown in Listing 9-2, add an ORDER BY clause to specify the sorting of the resultset. The *columnOrder* place-holder is a comma-separated list of columns to sort. The "ASC" or "DESC" option specified ascending or descending order; ascending is the default.

Note that this is optional per column, meaning that one column may be ordered ascending and the other descending. The following table shows examples of the ORDER BY clause with an explanation for each.

ORDER BY NAME	Simple statement to order by name with the default ascending (A-Z) sort
ORDER BY NAME DESC	Order by name but use descending (Z-A) order.
ORDER BY CATEGORYID, NAME	Order by CategoryID first, within each CategoryID order by Name.
ORDER BY CATEGORYID DESC, PRICE, NAME	Order by CategoryID first in descending order, then by price, then by Name. Price and Name use the default ascending sort order.

Figure 9-6. ORDER BY statements

More Advanced SQL

Thus far the queries have been run against a single table. This is rarely the case in practice and even can be shown in the above diagram – how often will the categoryID be known? In an application the user may be given drop-down choices with the name and when verifying the underlying data these names may be all that is known. For example, a typical question would be "show all products in the electronics category" rather than "show all products with category ID 2."

To pull information from more than one table a join is used. The basic syntax is shown below in Listing 9-3. The sections that follow will discuss the different types of joins and other operations on multiple tables and multiple result sets.

Listing 9-3. Basic Join syntax

```
SELECT columnlist FROM table1
JOIN table2 ON
column_t1 = column_t2
```

Given the above syntax, the following query would join the Product and category table:

Listing 9-4. First Join attempt

```
SELECT Name, Price, Description FROM
Product JOIN Category ON
categoryID = idCategory
```

While that certainly meets the syntax criteria in Listing 9-3, there is a serious problem – the query won't run. Any idea why?

The query won't run because the database can't properly resolve the Name and Description fields. Those fields exist in both the Product and Category tables and without any further clarification the columns are considered ambiguous.

One solution is to use the "proper name" of the column using the "dot syntax", which is "tablename.columnName," for example "Product.Name" to resolve the name. While this works it could potentially lead to a lot of redundant typing, especially if the number of columns retrieved is large. Also, if the column names were the same this same rule would apply to the ON clause; a join clause like that would be: JOIN ON Product.CategoryID = Category.CategoryID. Again, this works but could lead to a lot of redundant typing.

The preferred way to both remove the ambiguous naming and to shorten typing is with aliases. These work the same as the discussed in the SELECT section except now they apply to table names. Using aliases, the query in Listing 9-4 can be both expanded and properly written as

Listing 9-5. Proper Join query with aliases

```
SELECT p.Name, p.Price, c.Name, c.Description
FROM Product p JOIN Category c
ON p.categoryID = c.idCategory
```

This runs and produces a valid query. Also note that comparing these aliases to the aliases discussed earlier reveals that the AS keyword is optional. However, there are two Name columns which could be confusing to the end-user. Combining the above aliasing with the SELECT aliasing discussed earlier results in a query that is both simple to type and produces a more meaningful result set. This query is shown in Listing 9-6 and also adds a WHERE and ORDER BY to complete the query.

Listing 9-6. Final Join Query with aliases and conditions

```
SELECT p.Name 'Product Name'
,p.Price 'Product Price'
,c.Name 'Category Name'
,c.Description 'Category Description'
FROM Product p JOIN Category c
ON p.categoryID = c.idCategory
WHERE p.Price > 50
ORDER BY c.Name, p.Price
```

Note that the order of the statements - SELECT, FROM, JOIN, WHERE, ORDER BY – is important. There is one more common clause that, when present, comes after WHERE and before ORDER BY: GROUP BY.

GROUP BY is required when using aggregate functions in the SELECT column list. So far the columns have been returned as is, but SQL has many functions that can aggregate data such as MIN(), MAX(), and AVG(), among others. Columns that do not have an aggregate function must be present in the GROUP BY list. The following query shows how GROUP BY is used when finding the average price in each category.

Listing 9-7. Aggregate function and GROUP BY

```
SELECT AVG(p.Price) 'Average Price'
,c.Name 'Category Name'
,c.Description 'Category Description'
FROM Product p JOIN Category c
ON p.categoryID = c.idCategory
GROUP BY c.Name, c.Desription
```

The JOIN statements seen so far have actually been a shortcut for the full term of INNER JOIN. These joins produce results from two (or more) tables only when the specified JOIN condition is met. This is the desired behavior most of the time, but there can be occasions where items are desired that may or may not match. This type of join requires an OUTER JOIN. Essentially an OUTER JOIN is based on the concept of required values and optional values. This means that from one table all values that meet the criteria will be retrieved (the required table), and from the other table (the optional table) matching values may or may not be retrieved.

To specify which table is required and which is optional, the clauses LEFT OUTER JOIN and RIGHT OUTER JOIN are used; these are often abbreviated simply as LEFT JOIN and RIGHT JOIN. The meaning of LEFT and RIGHT indicate which side of the join contains the required table. To demonstrate, and example will be walked through to get the count of the number of Products in each Category.

To illustrate the Categorys, a simple SELECT is performed on the Category table. Both the simple query and the results are shown below.

Listing 9-8. The List of Cateogy records

```
SELECT Name FROM Category

Name
---------------------------
Auto Parts
Electronics
Kitchen
Home Office
Outdoor Living
Beauty Products
Household cleaning
```

The first attempt at getting the count or products in each Category is shown next. The COUNT() aggregate function is also introduced. Using the COUNT(*) syntax, it simple counts the number of records that match.

Listing 9-9. Counting the Products per Category

```
SELECT c.Name 'Category Name'
, COUNT(*) 'Num Products'
FROM Category c JOIN Product p
ON c.idCategory = p.CategoryID
GROUP BY c.Name
```

```
Category Name                        Num Products
---------------------------          ------------
Auto Parts                           7
Electronics                          10
Home Office                          11
Kitchen                              12
Outdoor Living                       7
```

This result is accurate, but it is incomplete. Comparing the Category list in the two queries reveals that there are two missing from the count query. This means that for those two categories, the condition c.idCategory = p.CategoryID doesn't match – there are no Products in that Category. Using an OUTER JOIN will properly reflect this in the result set, as shown in Listing 9-10. Also, the COUNT(p.Name) form is used for counting. This form only counts non-null values of the expression. Since a left join will have null for items that don't match, COUNT(p.Name) produces 0 for those rows.

Note the order of the tables and the OUTER JOIN – Category LEFT JOIN Product. Category is the "required" table and Product is the "optional" table. Using the COUNT() function works but doesn't necessarily show how the missing row is represented. The query/results in Listing 9-11 show how the database will put NULL into the result set when matching rows are not found.

Listing 9-10. LEFT JOIN for non-matching records

```
SELECT c.Name 'Category Name'
, COUNT(p.Name) 'Num Products'
FROM Category c LEFT JOIN Product p
ON c.idCategory = p.CategoryID
GROUP BY c.Name
```

```
Category Name                        Num Products
---------------------------          ------------
Auto Parts                           7
Beauty Products                      0
Electronics                          10
Home Office                          11
Household cleaning                   0
Kitchen                              12
Outdoor Living                       7
```

Another method for combining results is by using a UNION statement. This statement is meant to be used to combine similar result sets into one large result set. Logically this can thought of as "stacking" multiple results set together to form an end result. There are a few rules to adhere by:

- Result sets must have the same number of columns.

- Each column's data type must match.

- The first result set determines the column names.

- Only one ORDER BY statement is allowed and must follow the last result set.

- UNION will remove duplicate records in the result. If the duplicates are to remain, use the UNION ALL option.

Listing 9-11. OUTER JOIN results with NULL

```
SELECT c.Name 'Category'
, p.Name 'Product'
FROM Category c LEFT JOIN Product p
ON c.idCategory = p.CategoryID
WHERE c.Name LIKE 'Outdoor%'
OR c.Name LIKE 'House%'
ORDER BY c.Name
```

```
Category                      Product
--------------------          -----------------
Household cleaning            NULL
Outdoor Living                Patio Chair
Outdoor Living                Patio Table
Outdoor Living                Patio Umbrella
Outdoor Living                Gas Grill
Outdoor Living                Charcoal Grill
Outdoor Living                Fire Chimney
Outdoor Living                Soft sided pool
```

Again, the example given here will be overly simplified and is more to illustrate the syntax and end-result as opposed to the need for a UNION in this instance. The same results as using a UNION can often be found with a relational operation such as a JOIN with multiple WHERE conditions. However in some instances the results are easier to obtain in pieces, either because of the way the question was asked or because of the similarities in the conditions.

The query on the next page in Listing 9-12 shows the syntax for a UNION statement and the result set. The question asked is "Show the name and price of all items that have "USB" in the name and of all items that have "GB" in the name from the Electronics category. Note that not only are these two queries easily constructed on their own, they also pull information from different sources (one has a JOIN, the other does not).

Listing 9-12. UNION query

```
SELECT p.Name AS 'Product', p.Price
FROM Product p
WHERE p.Name LIKE '%USB%'
UNION
SELECT p.Name, p.Price
FROM Product p
JOIN Category c
ON p.CategoryID = c.idCategory
WHERE p.Name LIKE '%GB%'
AND c.Name = 'Electronics'
ORDER BY p.Price
```

```
Product                         Price
----------------------------    ---------------
4GB USB Thumb drive             8
8GB USB Thumb drive             14
20GB MP3 Player                 25
```

Another "building block" technique is the use of sub-queries. Essentially, a sub-query is simply a query within a query. It can be correlated, meaning that it refers to objects in the outer query, or uncorrelated, meaning that it does not refer to objects in the outer query. Sub-queries can appear most anywhere in a SQL expression and depending on where they appear they can assume different roles. For example, a sub-query that appears in a select list may result in a single value and behave like a column. A sub-query in a FROM list behaves like a virtual table and can be JOINed to and SELECTed from. In a WHERE clause the sub-query behaves like an expression and may result in a single value or list for comparison. The table in Figure 9-7 shows examples of sub-queries in each of these areas. In each, the sub-query is distinguished by italic font.

`SELECT c.Name AS 'Category Name'`
`, (SELECT COUNT(*)`
`  FROM Product p WHERE`
`  p.CategoryID = c.idCategory) AS`
`'Prod Count'`
`from Category c`
	Displays the Category Name and count of each product in that category. Note that this query is correlated because the sub-query refers to a column in the outer query.

`SELECT p.Name, p.Price FROM`
`Product p`
`JOIN (SELECT * FROM Category`
`     WHERE Name='Home Office')`
`  AS subCat`
`ON p.CategoryID =`
`subCat.idCategory`
`WHERE p.Name LIKE 'Desk%'`
	The sub-query acts as a virtual table named "subCat" that mimics the Product table with only the Category of "Home Office." This is then joined with the Product table resulting in items that start with "Desk" in the Home Office category.

`SELECT c.Name`
`FROM Category c`
`WHERE c.idCategory IN`
`( SELECT DISTINCT(CategoryID)`
`  FROM Product`
`  WHERE Name LIKE 'P%')`
	The sub-query produces a list of Category IDs that correspond to Products whose name begins with "P". (The DISTINCT operator removes duplicates; even though "Patio Chair" and "Patio Table" are both in category 5, only a single 5 will appear in the list.) The outer query then selects the Names of the categories that appear in the list.

Figure 9-7. *Example Sub-queries*

Again, these are simple queries and could be done other ways as well. But in each query think of the two-part thought process used to create one query, and then use that as part of another query.

So far the queries have mainly been between the Product and Category tables, or variations of them. In a practical application many more tables may be involved to fully retrieve the data that is desired. Even in the simple system shown in Figure 9-1 there can be the need to use information in many tables. The syntax and concepts shown thus far can be extended and/or combined to form more complex queries involving multiple tables and multiple concepts. The table in shows several queries that are more complex and are more representative of typical report queries.

```SELECT p.name AS 'Product'` `, p.Price, sp.Quantity` `FROM Product p` `JOIN Store_Product sp` `ON p.idProduct = sp.ProductID` `JOIN Store s` `ON s.idStore = sp.StoreID` `WHERE s.City = 'Charleston'```	Shows the Name, Price, and Quantity of each Product in the Charleston store.
```SELECT c.Name AS 'Category'` `, p.Name AS 'Product'` `, p.Price, sp.quantity` `FROM Product p JOIN category c` `ON p.CategoryID = c.idCategory` `JOIN Store_Product sp` `ON sp.ProductID = p.idProduct` `JOIN Store s` `ON s.idStore = sp.StoreID` `WHERE s.City='Prairie Town'` `ORDER BY c.Name, p.Name```	Same as above, but includes the category for each product and orders the results by category, then product.
```SELECT SUM(sp.Quantity) AS 'Number` `of Products'` `, c.Name AS 'Category'` `FROM Store_Product sp` `JOIN Store s` `ON s.idStore = sp.StoreID` `JOIN Product p` `ON p.idProduct = sp.ProductID` `JOIN Category c` `ON c.idCategory = p.CategoryID` `WHERE s.City = 'Prairie Town'` `GROUP BY c.Name```	Shows the total number of products for each category in the Prairie Town store.
```SELECT p.Name 'Product'` `, c.Name 'Category'` `FROM Product p JOIN Category c` `ON p.CategoryID = c.idCategory` `WHERE p.idProduct` `NOT IN (` ` SELECT sp.ProductID` ` FROM Store_Product sp` ` JOIN Store s` ` ON sp.StoreID = s.idStore` ` WHERE s.City = 'Prairie Town')```	Shows the Name and Category of the Products not found in the Prairie Town store.

Figure 9-8. *Multi-table queries*

While the sample creation and data-seeding scripts show the syntax for inserting data, there are two final statements for working with data: UPDATE and DELETE. This section will discuss both of these simple statements, along with an important concept that is important anytime data is being modified or deleted – transactions. Although standardized, syntax around starting a transaction is slightly different between database systems. Here MS SQL Server syntax will be used but this is easily translated into any other database system's syntax.

To modify data in a table, the following syntax is used:

Listing 9-13. UPDATE statement form

```
UPDATE table
SET column=value, column=value
WHERE condition
```

The *condition* term can specify one or more rows to update. For a single row the condition is typically based on the primary key column. If the condition results in multiple rows, all rows that match will be updated. Note that a sub-query can be used both in the condition query and to specify a value for updating.

The DELETE statement has the following syntax and similar rules apply to the condition statement: either one or multiple rows can be found to delete.

Listing 9-14. DELETE statement

```
DELETE FROM table
WHERE condition
```

Before discussing the syntax of a transaction, a brief definition is that a transaction is a single atomic unit of work. It can be a single statement or many statements, but anything defined in a transaction succeeds or fails as a whole. For a database this ensures consistency and integrity.

A typical example is when two dependent things are changed at once. In the example database, if the design was expanded to include sales information, both the recording of the sale of an item and its corresponding decrement in the Store_Product. Quantity column would need to be kept together to keep inventory and sales information consistent. Enclosing both operations in a single transaction would accomplish that goal.

Assuming there is StoreSales table, the process of inserting a new record into that table and decrementing the Quantity column is shown in Listing 9-15.

Listing 9-15. Transaction example

```
BEGIN TRAN
BEGIN
    INSERT INTO StoreSales (ProductID, SellDate, Amount)
    VALUES (24, '1-Aug-2012', 25.77)

    UPDATE Store_Product
    SET Quantity = Quantity - 1
    WHERE (ProductID = 24 AND StoreID = 4)
END

IF @@ERROR <> 0
    ROLLBACK
ELSE
    COMMIT
```

Again, this is a SQL script with SQL Server specific syntax. The @@ERROR statement is a SQL Server construct that detects errors on the server (such as a constraint violation or data type error); what is important to realize is that both the INSERT and UPDATE statement succeed or fail together. The decision to COMMIT or ROLLBACK can be error based, as above, or data based. Either way, the modification of data isn't finalized until either being committed or rolled back.

Programming Frameworks

The SQL statements discussed in the previous section were shown in the context of being directly connected to the database server via a dedicated client tool. This is fine for troubleshooting or inspecting data, but the majority of applications interact with a database through a data framework. These frameworks, such as JDBC and ADO.NET, provide programming constructs for working with relational data. An example of these statements were briefly seen in Chapter 5, but will be expanded on here.

One thing to note is that both JBDC and ADO.NET are frameworks, meaning that the interfaces and classes that compose them can be implemented by anyone. Often they are referred to as "drivers" implemented for a particular database. For example the "SQL Server JDBC driver" or the "MySQL ADO.NET driver" would refer to the set of Java classes for interacting with SQL Server and the .NET classes for interacting with MySQL.

While the terminology is slightly different between the libraries, the main concepts are the same. The major components and their purpose are listed below.

Connection – establishes and maintains the connection to the database.

Command – contains the SQL statement to execute.

ResultSet – a collection of the query results to be processed.

Exception – Driver-specific exceptions resulting from database operations.

The next several pages will show coding examples both in .NET and Java. Keep in mind that entire books are often dedicated to data framework programming; more in-depth resources are listed in the "suggested reading" section at the end of this book. The examples shown here will demonstrate basic operations leveraging the database discussed in the above SQL section along with reinforcing the need to be familiar with SQL syntax and constructs.

Basic ADO.NET

The ADO.NET driver for SQL Server is written by Microsoft and included in the .NET library. Other drivers for other databases are typically written by the database vendor. In this section, even though there is a SQL Express database for StoreInventory, the MySQL driver will be used to demonstrate the steps of wiring up a third party vendor's driver for use in .NET. Other than the initial steps of registering the library and the names of the concrete classes, the process for another provider (such as the built-in SQL Server or an Oracle ADO.NET provider) would be the same.

The MySql reference documentation should be consulted for installing the driver; in MySql terms this is referred to as "Connector/NET" and essentially consists of several assemblies (dlls) that need to be installed onto the development workstation. Once these assemblies are present, they simply need to be referenced in the project. This has been previously discussed in the UnitTest section (for nUnit) and the debugging section (for log4net). Adding the MySql reference to the project will result in the Solution explorer looking like Figure 9-9.

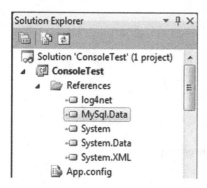

Figure 9-9. *Referencing the MySql assembly*

Once the assembly is added to the project the first thing to do is to import the proper namespaces. For the .NET library classes the base ADO.NET classes are defined in System.Data. The MySql specific implementation will be in the namespace MySql.Data.Client. From an implementation standpoint it is important to remember that to allow for different drivers, framework authors often use interfaces and base classes to expose functionality. This allows for loose-coupling and promotes the design of multiple layers of indirection so that switching implementation can be done with a minimal impact.

One important concept to all implementations is the connection string. This is the information provided to the driver to describe how to connect to the database. There are several options and different drivers may have different options, so it is important to review the driver documentation. However common to most are database server name, port, database name, and authentication information. The examples will show them declared as strings in the code; however in most applications these will be declared in configuration files or provided by other means so that the code can remain generic between different environments. As mentioned elsewhere in the book, it is very common to have development, testing, and production environments, each with dedicated database servers. Keeping the connection string in a configuration file means that the source code doesn't have to recompile between environments, only the configuration file changes.

The code in Listing 9-16 shows a function that queries the StoreInventory.Store table from the local database and prints the results to the console. The output is shown directly below.

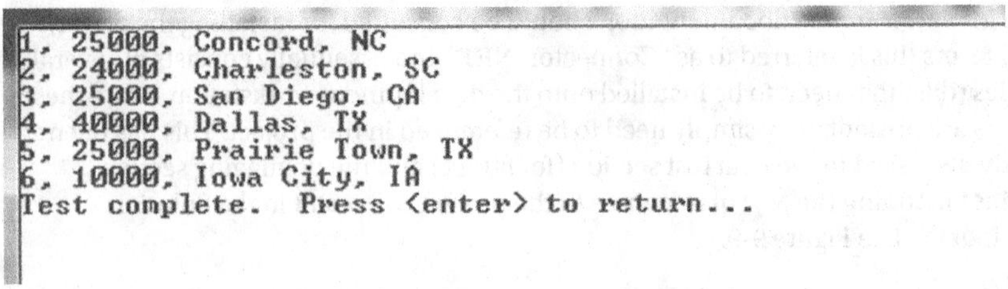

```
1, 25000, Concord, NC
2, 24000, Charleston, SC
3, 25000, San Diego, CA
4, 40000, Dallas, TX
5, 25000, Prairie Town, TX
6, 10000, Iowa City, IA
Test complete.  Press <enter> to return...
```

Figure 9-10. *Programmatic Query results*

Listing 9-16. Data Framework usage

```csharp
using System.Data;
using MySql.Data.MySqlClient;

public void GetAllStores()
{
    string strConnection = "Database=StoreInventory;" +
        "Data Source=localhost;" +
        "User Id=root;Password=password";

    IDbConnection conn = new MySqlConnection(strConnection);
    IDbCommand cmd = new MySqlCommand("Select * from Store");
    IDataReader dr = null;
    cmd.Connection = conn;
    try
    {
        int id, storeSqFt;
        string storeCity, storeState;
        conn.Open();
        dr = cmd.ExecuteReader();
        while (dr.Read())
        {
            id = dr.GetInt32(0);
            storeSqFt = dr.GetInt32(1);
            storeCity = dr.GetString(5);
            storeState = dr.GetString(6);
            Console.WriteLine(( id + ", " + storeSqFt) + ", " +
                                storeCity + ", " + storeState );
        }
    }
    catch (DbException dbe)
    {
        Console.WriteLine(dbe.StackTrace);
    }
```

```
finally
{
    if (dr != null)
        dr.Close();

    conn.Close();
}
}
```

Although simple the function in Listing 9-16 illustrates the core pattern of programmatic data framework usage. Several comments and important notes can be made concerning this code:

- Interface variables (IDbConnection, IDbCommand, etc) are used and are assigned objects that implement those particular interfaces (MySqlConnection, MySqlCommand, etc). This is the most flexible way, but also introduces a few restrictions. For example, the IDataReader Get... methods only allow for ordinal column specification as shown in the example. However most concrete DataReaders, such as MySqlDataReader, overload those methods to accept a string specification as well. If dr had been declared a MySqlDataReader then dr.GetString("City") could have been used.

- Note the use of "select *" in the query. This is actually inefficient over the wire because only four columns are being used in the function yet all are coming back. Based on the SQL SELECT discussion earlier, it is best to restrict the columns being returned. Note that if the columns are aliased and the overloaded Get... functions are used the strings must match the alias.

- IDataReader is a read-only, forward-only construct returned by the ExecuteReader call; this should be used anytime the query produces a result set. If a SQL statement is executed that does not return a result set, such as an UPDATE statement, ExecuteNonQuery, which returns an integer representing the number of rows affected, should be used.

- The results are looped over using the dr.Read() method which will return false when there are no more records to read.

- All database-related operations should be enclosed in try-catch blocks as a best-practice. In general these operations involve calls to remote servers or at the very least a call to another process, which can result in a multitude of errors including database timeouts, network failures, and permission errors.

- It is imperative to close the connection to the database. The safest place to do that is in the finally block as this will always be executed regardless of how the function is exited.

In straight SQL client queries the values to be searched on are frequently known or can be found through other direct queries, or the end result can be easily found in the produced record set. This is very seldom the case in programmatic SQL, usually because there is either input from the user or the result is expected to be a single result. To further filter queries through a programmatic interface, parameters are used. These consist of two parts; placeholders in the defined query whose values are replaced by the framework, and the definition of parameter objects that will be used to pass in the desired values.

Rather than returning all stores, how would the code in Listing 9-16 look if it was changed to allow for dynamic input for filtering on store size? Below is a snippet containing only the changed code, the rest of the function remains the same.

Listing 9-17. Using a parameter

```
IDbCommand cmd = new MySqlCommand("Select * from Store where " +
                                  "SquareFeet >= @sqft");
IDbDataParameter parm = new MySqlParameter("@sqft",
                                           MySqlDbType.Int32);
parm.Direction = ParameterDirection.Input;
parm.Value = 25000;  // normally supplied by user choice
cmd.Parameters.Add(parm);
```

In keeping with the interface usage of the rest of the code, the IDbDataParameter interface is being used, instantiated by a MySqlParameter object. The "@sqft" notation is the named parameter that will be replaced. Notice that the name given to the MySqlParameter constructor matches that name. Each driver and/or database can have a naming convention or requirement for parameters; some match solely by position so it is important to know the specifics for the chosen driver/database combination.

In the example, the value is hard-coded as 25000, so the query will return all stores that have a size greater-than or equal to 25000. In a typical application this value could be selected from a drop-down or a numeric input field, and then used to set the Value. The results are shown in Figure 9-11.

```
1, 25000, Concord, NC
3, 25000, San Diego, CA
4, 40000, Dallas, TX
5, 25000, Prairie Town, TX
Test complete.  Press <enter> to return...
```

Figure 9-11. *Result using a parameterized query*

Basic JDBC

Java JDBC usage has a similar construct. In the case of MySQL the driver is known as "Connector/J" and is downloadable as a single JAR file. After putting it on the classpath, the same query as shown in ADO.NET in Listing 9-16 is shown using Java and JDBC on the next page in Listing 9-18. The output is exactly the same.

The first call inside the try, Class.forName(), is the manner in which the class is loaded into the project. This can be configured in other types of Java applications (such as a web container) but the safest way for a test console application is to include the MySQL JAR file in the classpath, then load it using forName().

In similar fashion to using the .NET interfaces, in the Java code the JDBC Interfaces Connection, Statement, and ResultSet are used. The DriverManager class takes care constructing the appropriate concrete objects once the getConnection method is supplied with a connection string. Note that JDBC connection string has a different form than the ADO.NET connection string. Again, its important to realize that even though things are consistent within a framework and the overall end result is the same, the framework themselves may have subtle differences. In addition to the different connection string format, also notice that the column references in JDBC are 1-based, whereas in ADO.NET they were 0-based.

Listing 9-18. JDBC Usage example

```java
import java.sql.Connection;
import java.sql.DriverManager;
import java.sql.ResultSet;
import java.sql.SQLException;
import java.sql.Statement;

public void getSomeData() throws Exception
{
    Connection conn = null;
    Statement stmt = null;
    ResultSet rs = null;

    try
    {
        Class.forName("com.mysql.jdbc.Driver").newInstance();
        conn = DriverManager.getConnection(
"jdbc:mysql://localhost/StoreInventory?user=root&password=password");
        stmt = conn.createStatement();
        rs = stmt.executeQuery("SELECT * FROM Store");

        while(rs.next())
        {
            System.out.println(rs.getInt(1) + ", " +
                                rs.getInt(2) + ", " +
                                rs.getString(6) + ", " +
                                rs.getString(7));
        }
    }
    catch(SQLException se)
    {
        System.out.println(se.getMessage());
    }
```

```
finally
{
    rs.close();
    conn.close();
}
}
```

Finally, the parameterized statement for JDBC is shown below in Listing 9-19. Note that unlike the ADO.NET example, a different class is used for parameterized statements than for non-parameterized statements. In the example different parameter syntax is followed and position order is used for the parameter. Again, only the code that changed is shown.

Listing 9-19. Changes for a parameterized JDBC call

```
// an additional import
import java.sql.PreparedStatement;

    // instead of Statement
    PreparedStatement stmt = null;

        // Instead of createStatement
        stmt = conn.prepareStatement(
            "SELECT * FROM Store where squarefeet >= ?");
        // Set the value of the parameter
        stmt.setInt(1, 25000);
```

Object-Relational Mapping – Methods and Tools

The frameworks discussed in the previous sections suffer from what is commonly referred to as an "impedance mismatch" – that is relational set data being used by an object oriented language. Many manual solutions to this exist, the very simplest of which is to manually create new objects while looping through the result set and maintain those new objects in a collection class.

For example, to represent the StoreInventory database, a domain class would be created to model each data table – Store, Product, and Category with the appropriate members. This would commonly be modeled in a "Data Access Layer" and would typically be filled with methods for returning Lists of objects bases on parameters, IDs, specific search conditions, or even all objects in a table. Listing 9-20 shows the .NET code to manually map from a record set returned by a query to a List of domain objects.

Listing 9-20. Manual object mapping

```
using System.Data;
using MySql.Data.MySqlClient;
using System.Collections.Generic;
using Domain.Model.Product;
```

```
public List<Product> GetAllProducts()
{
    List<Product> prods = new List<Product>();
    IDbConnection conn = new MySqlConnection(_strConnection);
    IDbCommand cmd = new MySqlCommand("Select * from Product");
    IDataReader dr = null;
    cmd.Connection = conn;
    try
    {
        int id, catId;
        string prodName, prodDesc;
        float price;

        conn.Open();
        dr = cmd.ExecuteReader();
        while (dr.Read())
        {
            id = dr.GetInt32(0);
            prodName = dr.GetString(1); price = dr.GetFloat(2);
            catId = dr.GetInt(3); prodDesc = dr.GetString(4);

            Product p = new Product(id, prodname, price,
                                    catId, prodDesc);

            prods.add(p);
        }
    }
    catch (DbException dbe) {}

    finally { // cleanup code here }

    return prods;
}
```

Recently a large push has been made to remove the need for manual mapping and have complete frameworks available for mapping. These are known in general as Object-Rational Mapping (ORM) tools and frameworks. Some of the more popular ones are Entity Framework (for .NET) and Hibernate (for Java) although there are several that exist for each language and many more for other languages. A full discussion is beyond the scope of this book; several books are listed in the suggested reading and are dedicated entirely to these technologies.

At a very high level, the emphasis has been on allowing the developer to annotate POCOs (Plain Old CLR Objects) and POJOs (Plain Old Java Objects) with specific annotations and/or use specific conventions that will then allow their respective frameworks to handle all the behind-the-scenes mapping. Given these conventions, it is entirely possible to create a fully functional application, complete with a database, while never actually writing a SQL query or touching the database server.

The code in Listing 9-21 shows a very basic example of annotating a class to represent the Store object so that the chosen data framework can map it appropriately.

Listing 9-21. Simple POCO annotation

```
[Table (Name="StoreInventory.Store")]
public class Store
{
    [Column(IsPrimaryKey = true)]
    public int idStore;

    [Column(CanBeNull = false)]
    public int SquareFeet;

    [Column(CanBeNull = false)]
    public String StoreType;

    [Column(CanBeNull = false)]
    public String City;

    // other columns here...
}
```

The example is in .NET LINQ to SQL, but other frameworks have similar mapping strategies. Frameworks and tools are constantly evolving with the constant aim being to improve both model performance and ease of development. Microsoft Entity Framework and Java Hibernate are among the most popular at the time of this writing.

With this push it has also been imperative to bring querying into the programming language as a natural extension. This allows a developer to write a SQL-like query within the language (.NET or JAVA) and have that translated by the framework to the appropriate real SQL query. In the Microsoft world this is known as LINQ (Language Integrated Query); Hibernate has HQL (Hibernate Query Language). Both of these allow for querying collections and objects using object syntax, the frameworks handle the necessary translation to SQL and return objects or a collection of objects.

To illustrate how language query syntax looks, an object query is shown in Listing 9-22 to query for a list of Stores with SquareFeet greater than or equal to 25000. This query has the same output as Figure 9-11. While this is LINQ, other object query languages such as HQL have similar syntax and capabilities.

The key piece is the DataContext class. This is a .NET Framework class and can be used directly as in the example, but is also often derived from during the building of the model code to expose the user-defined POCO objects as properties. In the case of Listing 9-22, the generic function GetTable is used in conjunction with the generic class Table to produce a Table<Store> object. This object is then used in the object query referencing the object's properties. Internally, the DataContext handles the mapping between the object world and the SQL world using the POCO annotations to produce a SQL query and handle the mapping of the values upon return.

Listing 9-22. Sample Object query

```
// Framework class to manage connections, map objects, etc.
DataContext context = new DataContext(connectionString);

Table<Store> sList = context.GetTable<Store>();

List<Store> bigStoreList = (from s in sList
                            where s.SquareFeet >= 25000
                            select s).ToList();

foreach (var s in bigStoreList)
    Console.WriteLine("{0}, {1}, {2}, {3}",
                      s.idStore, s.SquareFeet, s.City, s.StoreState);
```

Summary

Structured Query Language (SQL) is instrumental in examining relational data. Whether directly through a client interface tool or through a programming framework, SQL remains the primary tool for working with data. Recent developments in Object Relational Mapping tools and language specific enhancements have started to move the bar towards this area and provide a viable and efficient alternative to manually dealing with the impedance mismatch between relational data and object-oriented languages. This discussion, while rather lengthy, has really just touched the surface, especially in the area of ORM tools and frameworks. The reader is encouraged to consult the Appendix for additional resources and to explore more by coding using a framework and/or ORM tool suite.

■ ■ ■

Enterprise Considerations and Other Topics

There are several factors that differ in an enterprise environment from an educational environment. Depending on the size and structure of the university or college some of these factors may be experienced to some degree. We will briefly list these concerns from a large organizational perspective and how each impacts or influences software development. We also discuss some general topics related to the software development career.

These topics may also be used to form the a basis for some interview questions – when the interviewer asks "Do you have any questions for me?" asking a question based on one or more of the following topics can show that you are thinking in a large organization frame of mind.

One final disclaimer – the discussions in this section are based loosely on the experiences of the author and several of the author's colleagues; software professionals with an average of 15 years of experience. This means most of us have seen the dot-com boom, bust, and what has happened since. Most have been in large organizations (hundreds or thousands of employees total), "micro shops" (3-4 developers and a dozen total employees), and all sizes in between. Employment trends, technology trends, and business practices constantly change, so the discussions forthcoming should not be taken as an absolute predictor of how technology employment will be like, only as a general survey of some topics that are not often discussed in an academic setting.

Number and Location of Team Members and/or Users

In large organizations and today's job climate it is becoming more and more common for team members to be geographically dispersed. Several factors influence this trend – non-local company acquisitions, availability of talent in specific areas, cost of real-estate, and even security. Collaboration tools such as GoToMeeting and Microsoft Live Meeting make distributed team communication easier than ever; webinars and other distributed learning technologies reduce the need for travel expenditures. All this increasingly means that companies are becoming more and more willing to find talent wherever it is located rather than insisting it be local to the company.

Likewise, end users can be located just about anywhere. For business software locations such as New York, Los Angeles, and Hong Kong are important. This has to be taken into account for not only software response times (such as a user in Hong Kong receiving a file from the States or calling a web service based in Omaha) but for software maintenance as well. Upgrading a system at midnight Eastern Time is noon in Hong Kong; Asian users may be slightly upset if there system goes offline in the middle of their business day.

Game programmers are especially affected by distant users. Increasingly, multi-player games can be attended from anywhere with a wide range of broadband speeds and response times to factor in. This could have a huge effect on performance and must be taken into account. The important thing is to remember this when developing and testing and to attempt to simulate remote users with built-in delays, random communication failures, etc.

System Integration

Unlike legacy client-server systems, most modern applications rely on many components for information. In addition to the multi-tier architecture discussed in Chapter 7:, systems may have to interface with other systems via web services, remote method calls, DCOM, or some type of messaging. This has profound impact on applications, for two main reasons. One, there is a possibility that the external system may be unreachable for some reason. And two, the external system may change its interface or data format without proper communication. Error handling, retrying, and alternate processing strategies are very important when dealing with external systems. Also, designing systems via dependency injection allow for testing of these interfaces without actually connecting to them. This allows both for positive testing (aka "happy case"), when communication goes right, and for negative testing, or simulating when communication goes wrong.

Separation of Duties and Environmental Limitations

In larger software organizations there are typically several stages software goes through before being released to the customer, internal or external. These different stages will have different limits on how software developers can interact with each environment. The reasons for this separation are very diverse. In some cases, such as retail software, there is no way to provide developers access to end user's desktops, so "production access" is a moot point. In other situations where the "customer" is an internal user, production access for developers is limited for security and risk reasons. The time card application from the last chapter is a good example of an internal application where access to production needs to be restricted; both for security of personal information and the possibility of fraud. For the following discussion the assumption is an internal application that is never seen by users outside the organization but still has sensitive data. This could be human resources software such as our time card application or an application that processes outside user data but isn't seen by them directly - a policy analyzer for an insurance company for example. In this situation, many organizations will have a minimum of three different environments for the software – development, testing, and production.

In development, software developers may have complete access and authority to their application. This usually includes the right to install and change application code, run tests, browse logs and directory configurations, edit files, etc. However there could be restrictions on what is allowed to be done or tools to be used; not so much for the development environment itself but to align the system with what is allowed or prohibited in the higher environments. So even though a developer can change application code, they may not be allowed to apply service packs or patches to the operating system.

Development environments are also typically matched with development areas in supporting services, such as a database or a messaging system. And although software developers may have elevated privileges to these supporting environments (relative to production), they are still most likely owned and managed by different teams. Although privileges are greater than the higher environments there could still be limitations. For example, a software developer may have rights to execute certain SQL statements in the development database, such as creating a table, but would not have permission to create the actual database. This would be restricted to the database team and any database creation would have to be requested.

The testing environment is probably the most diverse area in terms of developer rights. In some organizations testing is only slightly different from development; developers have rights to install software and review logs but cannot edit files or directory structure. Developers may also work directly with individual testers to step through testing and fix defects (bugs) on the fly. This could pose a problem however if the developer is not diligent about keeping the code in development up to date. Many organizations have deemed this strategy too risky and no longer operate in this fashion.

Many organizations now treat the testing environment as "pre-production" and allow very limited or even no developer access. In these cases dedicated support teams would use installation programs or other tools to install the application and the developer would have no access to tweak the installation, directly review logs or files, or modify code. The users at this stage are the Quality Assurance (QA) team; the group that takes the original business requirements and exercises the application to ensure all the requirements are met. They would test the application for a specific period of time, and then produce a list of defects. This list would be given to developers who would work on them in the development environment before having the code re-installed in the testing environment. In this process it is important that the code remain unchanged while the testers are testing because they are in effect simulating end users.

The production environment is typically completely inaccessible to developers. The application is installed and monitored by dedicated teams with no access to the source code. These teams also work with the other support services, such as a production database team or system administrators, to troubleshoot any end user issues. They may have access to the log files or other diagnostic information to send to developers. In this environment this is typically the only way developers have to diagnose a problem.

Software Political Statements- Which Language/Platform is Better?

The examples in this book have been mostly in Java and C# with a tiny bit of C++. Are these the only languages out there? Of course not, but they seem to be the most common in educational institutions. All are based on a similar C-like syntax and the examples should be easily translated. According to (Tiobe, 2011) the top five languages in the software community by popularity are Java, C, C++, PHP, and C#. This often generates the question from students "Which language should I learn?" In my experience the best possible answer is "As many as you can."

While there have been periods of "language wars", i.e. "C++ vs. Java", ".NET vs. Java", and several bold predictions that a certain language will rule the world, the practical truth is that many organizations, especially large ones, may use several different and competing languages and technologies under the same roof. And while there are probably still rivalries amongst the teams, the truth is that pleasing the business users or end customers is much more important than using a specific technology. Often times the choice is dictated by components that are already in place, such as a feed by a legacy system that uses a technology that integrates easily with a specific platform. The end user usually does not care about technology nearly as much as getting the desired results.

There are many opportunities to expand into programming languages other than what is taught in school or other than what is currently being used. Many tools are available for free or are fairly inexpensive. C++ has several free editors and IDEs such as Code::Blocks and the Eclipse CDT. There are also several libraries available to supplement the latest C++ standard; everything from embedded control libraries to cross-platform GUI libraries.

For Java, again the Eclipse platform is available for free, as is Netbeans – both are capable of writing, compiling, and debugging Java applications. Many plug-ins exist for expanding their capability to include server-side web programming, AJAX applications, etc. Application servers such as JBoss and Apache are also free and allow investigation into multi-tiered web and service applications.

Microsoft's Express editions are free (registration required) and include VB, C#, C++, and a web developer edition. These allow for gaining experience in the Microsoft development environment and are targeted at the hobbyist developer. They also have an "advanced mode" that allow for menus and options to be very similar to the professional editions of Visual Studio; this is meant to ease transition from these free editions to the professional release.

There are also free database platforms, MySQL being the most popular. Tool sets are also available that allow integration with Java, .NET, and C++ applications. There is a management studio available that allows for management of the database server and for writing queries. Many online hosting sites use MySQL and offer various web-based management tools as well.

Both Oracle and Microsoft offer "Express" and "developer" editions of their database platforms. These allow for personal development or relatively small applications to use a SQL database that is in m any ways comparable to the full scale product. Also, in recent years lightweight database systems and structured storage systems are becoming increasingly popular. These are generally server-less file-based systems that can enforce SQL structures such as foreign-key relationships, in the case of SQL-like systems, or structured data relationships that is not based on SQL, sometimes referred to as NoSQL systems. There are many of these but some of the more popular are SQLite, which is used in many mobile platforms but also has a desktop API; Derby, which is a Java based SQL-like database; and RavenDB, which is a NoSQL document storage engine. Again, these are few among many and all options should be thoroughly researched prior to implementation.

Mobile development is also an area that offers many free or low-cost tools to expand development skills. Android programs are written (mostly) in Java and a development kit is free for download as is a plug-in for Eclipse that includes a graphical design environment and simulator. Microsoft has an Express Phone developer platform for Windows Phone 7 – this technology revolves around C# and Silverlight. Apple allows iPhone development for a small fee ($99 yearly at the time of this writing) and is arguably the most complex environment; Objective-C is an object-oriented version of standard C.

PHP, as mentioned above, is still one of the most popular web-centric languages. It is mainly a set of special-purpose HTML-like tags, but has also gained many object oriented faculties in recent releases. Included are built-in function calls for using a MySQL database, and it neatly integrates with several web server platforms including Apache. Many IDEs, including Eclipse and Netbeans, have PHP plug-ins that are tailored for PHP. Also, normal editors such as Notepad can be used; some text editors such as SciTE or Notepad++ also provide syntax highlighting for PHP functions and keywords.

There is another thing to keep in mind regarding software and enterprise environments. In enterprise environments, especially very large enterprises, changes in software have the ability to impact a great number of dependent systems. This can be true with vendor components or in-house components. Also, dependent software such as the back-end database(s) or messaging middleware may be handled by a separate team that is on their own upgrade schedule. The result of this is that technology in large systems and organizations (or even small systems or organizations that interface to a large number of other systems) may not keep pace with the speed of innovation in the industry. For example, in early 2012 as this is being written the current version of the Microsoft .NET framework is 4.0. The latest Java release is 1.7 and the JBoss Application Server is at version 7.1. However in the author's world and the world of several colleagues, those using .NET are usually using version 3.0 or 3.5. In a few extreme cases some have just recently ported Visual Basic 6 applications to .NET even though VB6 was replaced by .NET 1.0 in 2002. Those using Java are most often using some version of 1.6; those using JBoss are split between releases 5 and 6. So the most common scenario is one to two versions behind.

Again, the previous paragraph should be read with the standard disclaimer of "your experiences may vary greatly" because so much depends on the organization itself. Some software houses may be small or agile enough to stay on the cutting edge. Some may even specialize in this "cutting edge" area and provide services to larger, slower moving companies.

Software Libraries and Frameworks – Use Third Party or Write In-House?

This discussion follows the language discussion because it is just about as controversial. Several factors including maturity of the library, knowledge of the developers, size of the team, previous team experience, and even corporate policy can determine the answer to this question. In some cases, specialized hardware for instance, a third-party library may be required. In other cases corporate policy restricts third-party libraries to only those that have been approved. This may be due to perceived security risk or simply a general desire to keep the code base uniform. It usually does not make sense for different libraries to be used on different projects. There also may already be an in-house library that addresses the need. The discussion here is when given an option, what are the pros and cons of each answer?

In general, if there is a library that addresses a particular need and it is approved for use it should be used. If there is a case where multiple libraries that fulfill the same need are approved, then the decision would be based on personal experience or team experience. In most cases the use of an established library results in better productivity, fewer bugs, and more maintainable code.

From a career perspective the use of third-party libraries can be a double-edged sword. On one hand, if the library is a commonly used established industry standard then the experience gained by using the library is desirable and the knowledge would be very transferable on a job-to-job basis. At the time of this writing some examples of libraries and frameworks like this would be jQuery, Spring, and ASP.NET MVC.

On the other hand, if a library or framework is extremely useful but is not widely used then the career impact of it can be neutral or even negative. Spending four years working with a framework that is not very popular only serves to enhance the marketability of the base language. For example, a developer that spends several years using the BigBadGuiTools Java library may find it difficult to apply that experience when looking for the next job that uses a more mainstream library. The basic concepts are probably similar, but compared to another candidate who has used the mainstream library all along, the BigBadGuiTools (BBGT) developer would most likely be at a disadvantage. At best the developer could become an expert in BBGT and apply that knowledge in a limited niche market but may end up having to learn the mainstream library after all. In that case the time with BBGT only enhanced the developer's Java skills.

In-house libraries and frameworks can be great learning experiences and are sometimes necessary due to the diverse usage and nature of software. In many cases combining a custom in-house library with domain knowledge (see next section) can greatly enhance a developer's curb appeal, both to their current company and also to other companies with a similar product or service. Care must be taken of course not to become too esoteric and fall into the BBGT trap as mentioned in the previous section.

Domain Knowledge

Writing good software from a technical perspective is important. Frequently overlooked however is the importance of knowing the "domain", the user-knowledge area where the software will be used. Though this is not always a necessity, in many situations it can help the developer write software that is easier to use. Looking at software from a user perspective may challenge the developer to simplify the interface to a complex system.

In many industries the terminology is important and is usually a baseline requirement for understanding a business even if in-depth knowledge of the underlying processes is not. Banking, insurance, retail, advertising, and real estate are examples of areas that have their own set of terms. Knowing the terms of a particular domain not only can make designing and developing the software easier (because it is easier to communicate with the users) but can also help the developer become valuable in a particular field.

Continuing Education

As mentioned above in the discussion on software, the speed of technology and programming tool innovation is usually much faster than the speed of adoption of these tools, especially in larger companies. To stay relatively current in these situations is the responsibility of the individual. Some have suggested that a programmer should be willing to spend approximately five hours a week keeping up with technology (Wake, 2002). Trade magazines, online blogs, dedicated topic web sites, and product following on social networking are but a few ways to stay abreast of industry trends. Below is a more local way, but the ways to keep current in technology is almost as numerous as the number of different technologies.

Local User Groups are typically excellent forums for keeping abreast of current trends and technologies. Typically these fall into a couple categories: technology or product. There may be a Java User Group, an Oracle User Group, or a Dot Net User group on the technology side, or a SharePoint or WebSphere User Group on the product side. Meeting schedules and times vary but are typically once a month during the evening as participation and presentations are conducted by industry professionals. Occasionally all-day weekend events, known as "Code Camps" or "Product Days" may be held where several speakers and/or presenters will not only demonstrate the latest technologies, but participants can have hands-on sessions to experience it for themselves.

These user groups are sometimes sponsored by local IT companies or recruiting firms and typically are attended heavily by local professionals. So not only are they opportunities to keep abreast of the latest trends and technologies, they are also excellent networking opportunities. Word of mouth is often times a better job hunting method than online or by other means. Additionally, if the sponsor is an IT recruiting firm, their current opportunities are often presented by a recruiter; talking with a recruiter face-to-face at a user group is an excellent way to establish report as a job seeker.

Contractor or Full Time Employee?

First, let me define each term. A "contractor" is someone who works for a placement agency and has an assignment at a customer of the agency. A "full time employee" (FTE or "perm") is a normal employee of a company and does work on the company's behalf. So which is better? As with so many other questions in life, the answer is a resounding "it depends." Salary is only one consideration when evaluation the type of employment.

Also, let me reiterate the section disclaimer. The statements below are based solely on the experiences of the author and some of his colleagues. They should not be taken as absolute fact or an absolute gauge of what to expect in each situation. These are general statements that merely should be points of consideration when deciding on employment. Your mileage may vary greatly.

Generally speaking, contractors get paid a higher hourly rate. However the placement agency may or may not provide benefits such as insurance or holiday pay. Paying for insurance and not getting paid for vacation can be a large expense and/or loss of income. A contractor can also be terminated at any time with no severance or advanced warning. The agency or the customer may also place limits on overtime or hours in general. Finally, many companies place limits on the amount of time a contractor can be employed at a single location, such as 12 or 18 months. As mentioned above, contractors may also stay more current in their technology toolset because of the relatively frequent job changing and need to stay highly competitive.

Full time employees are generally paid less than contractors when comparing hourly rate, but the difference is usually in benefits such as insurance, vacation, and (usually) better job security. Depending on the company there may be additions to base pay such as bonuses or profit-sharing. In general FTE's are also eligible for severance packages along with out-placement assistance if being displaced. Other perks may include training and career advancement opportunities that aren't offered to non-FTE staff. One of the downsides is "technology stagnation", as mentioned above. Being on a single team or product may limit technology growth if the product is slow moving compared to the speed of new technology integration.

Summary

Enterprise situations are typically quite different from education scenarios. Distributed users, multiple teams and platforms, and segregated environments require a somewhat different approach to software solutions. Hopefully the brief discussions in this section will highlight some of the differences and introduce students to an enterprise thought process. Again, some of these topics may have been experienced in school but often the extent to which they impact development is minimal compared to their influence in the corporate world.

Physical enterprise considerations are also just one aspect of professional development. Arguably the pace of new tool and technology introduction in software development is as fast as any field in the world. And certainly the range of application software is even outgrowing Duct Tape. Keeping up with this pace is daunting but also can be very rewarding.

■ ■ ■

Discussion Questions

This appendix will provide some discussion sections and problems for each part. Most of them will be essay or discussion in nature; the intent is to help the reader think about each topic in terms of how it may be presented in an interview or discussed in a team atmosphere. Some interviews consist of small programming problems; this type of question may also be presented as a small assignment that might asked in a typical interview or a small prototyping project.

Chapter 1: Version Control

1. What is the purpose of version control?

2. Describe the two most common strategies for file locking.

3. What are the advantages and disadvantages for each strategy in 2)?

4. Is version control workstation- or server-based?

5. Describe how conflicts occur. Which file-locking strategy helps to prevent conflicts? How is it minimized in the other strategy?

6. What are three types of version control interface tools?

7. Describe the tools and processes used to resolve conflicts.

8. How does tagging and branching work? What is each used for?

9. What type of files should NOT be kept in the repository?

The answer to the question in Figure 1-34: This is a revision graph in TortoiseCVS. At version 1.20 of the file it was realized there was some functionality introduced that was no longer needed. The changes were very extensive and removing them as a unit would be very time consuming. However there were also some bug fixes in versions 1.17 and 1.19 that were important but could be redone easily. So the strategy was to branch the code at 1.16 into a branch called "working_ni_16". The bug fixes were made and checked in to the repository resulting in version 1.16.2.1. After this version was tested and found to be good, the version 1.16.2.1 completely replaced version 1.20 and became version 1.21 in the main trunk. Note that this last operation, replacing the trunk with a branch, was done from the command line as the command syntax was actually clearer then the GUI plug-in method to do the same operation.

Chapter 2: Unit Testing and Test Driven Development

1. Who does unit testing? Is it different from user testing?

2. Do unit tests have to touch every single piece of code?

3. What legacy testing process did unit testing replace?

4. Name three popular unit testing tools.

5. Define mock objects and their role in test driven development.

6. Describe how unit testing can be a part of continuous integration.

7. How do unit tests help with refactoring?

8. Does test driven development ensure bug-free code?

9. How does test driven development promote simple code?

10. How does unit testing and test driven development affect the design of the overall software system?

Chapter 3: Refactoring

1. What is the purpose of refactoring?

2. Can or should refactoring change the outward facing interface of existing code?

3. List six different types of refactorings and describe the purpose for each.

4. If there are large segments of repeated code, or nearly repeated code, what is the refactoring that can be applied?

5. While refactoring the code is it a good idea to do bug fixing at the same time? Why or why not?

6. What technique is often combined with refactoring to make sure the refactorings do not change the code?

7. List the problems with the method on the next page, and then note the steps to refactor it.

(HINT – if you actually refactor it, don't forget to write a unit test first).

```
public Double DoTest(string s)
{
    string nex = "Database=test;Data Source=localhost;
                  User Id=root;Password=password";
    int c = 0;
    double d = 0.0;
    double sal = 0.0;
    MySqlConnection conn = new MySqlConnection(nex);
    MySqlCommand cmd = new MySqlCommand("Select id, firstname,
                                         lastname, " +
     "salary from customers where jobtitle " + "like " + s + "%");
    MySqlDataReader dr = null;
    cmd.Connection = conn;
    try
    {
        int id;
        String s1;
        string s2;
        conn.Open();
        dr = cmd.ExecuteReader();
        int nCounter = 0;
        while (dr.Read())
        {
            id = dr.GetInt32(0);
            s1 = dr.GetString(1);
            s2 = dr.GetString(2);
            sal += dr.GetDouble(3);
            Console.WriteLine((id +", "+s2)+", "+s1+": " + sal);
            nCounter++;
            d = sal / nCounter;
        }
        c=nCounter;
        return d;
    }
    catch (MySqlException mse)
    {
        Console.WriteLine("Error while connecting
                           to the database!");
    }
    finally
    {
        if (dr != null)
        dr.Close();
        conn.Close();
    }
    return 0.0d;
}
```

Chapter 4: Build Tools and Continuous Integration

1. What is the difference between a compiler and a build tool?

2. Define the terms: target, property, action, and convention-over-configuration.

3. Explain the difference between a make file and an Ant build file.

4. What are three ways a continuous integration server can be triggered to produce a build?

5. What else can a continuous integration tool do besides compile code?

6. Explain how build tools can insulate a developer from dependent library changes.

7. What is the difference between a build tool and a continuous integration tool?

8. Where can a build tool reside? Where does a continuous integration tool most often reside?

9. How does continuous integration reduce overall project risk?

10. Name two other tools that the continuous integration can use?

11. How are configuration files used in deploying to multiple environments?

12. Can a program be made aware of its runtime environment and configure itself to use appropriate settings?

13. Name 4 things that are often different among different runtime environments.

Chapter 5: Debugging

1. Define the following terms: step-over, step-through, step-out.

2. What is a break point? What are some of the options when setting a breakpoint?

3. What is required for remote debugging?

4. Describe the tools that are available for logging.

5. Compare and contrast logging and debugging.

6. List three different places to write log entries to and list the pros and cons of each one.

7. What is the call stack?

8. How are the following tools used - "Immediate window", "Locals", and "Watch Window"?

9. Can a debugger be used on the production release?

Chapter 6: Development Methodologies

1. Explain how story points in Agile map to work hours

2. Can Extreme Programming practices be used within a waterfall project?

3. According to Scrum, should the developer use the XP development process?

4. Who typically leads and manages a waterfall project? A Scrum project?

5. Explain the concept of sprints and frequent releases.

6. List four types of meetings held by a Scrum team and what they are used for.

7. Compare waterfall and Scrum in terms of flexibility and release cycles.

8. What is pair-programming and how it is used?

9. What are coding standards, collective code ownership, and daily builds? Are they specific to one type of development methodology?

Chapter 7: Design Patterns and Architecture

1. Explain the difference between logical architecture and physical architecture.

2. Name two patterns that derive from the MVC pattern and how they differ from MVC.

3. List three advantages of using design patterns.

4. Explain the roles of the Model, the View, and the Controller in the MVC pattern.

5. What pattern does the foreach loop (in Java and C#) make use of? (HINT: it was not discussed in this book.)

6. List 5 examples of the Observer pattern and name the observer and publisher.

7. What are three advantages of using the Inversion of Control pattern? How do these help in enterprise development?

8. Research how patterns such as MVP and MVVM have expanded upon the MVC pattern and what their major differences are.

9. Explain why refactoring to patterns, although appearing to be more complex, is actually beneficial.

10. How can coding to interfaces be used when refactoring existing components?

11. Explain how refactoring with patterns can help save prototyping efforts.

12. Explain why load-balanced web servers cannot store session state in their local memory.

13. Describe the purpose of logical to physical architecture mapping.

14. Does having multiple environments such as production and disaster recovery affect the physical architecture diagram? What can the diagram be used for in this case?

Chapter 8: Software Requirements

1. Name two groups that make use of the business requirements of a system.

2. Business requirements are used as a basis for what development document?

3. Discuss if or how formal requirements documents can be used in an Agile software project.

4. What is the target audience for each type of requirement document?

5. Once each requirements document has been finalized, what happens if a new requirement is discovered?

6. For requirements concerning changes to an existing system, are bug fixes and feature requests appropriate to include? In which document(s)?

7. Describe how business requirements coordinate with developer unit testing. How about functional requirements?

8. What is the traceability matrix?

9. If a project has a requirements document with 63 requirements and by the release date there have been 41 change control items, is that a problem?

Chapter 9: Just Enough SQL

1. Name and describe the two main JOIN types.

2. Are column aliases ever required?

3. Explain the purposes of aliases.

4. Describe the special steps to take when using an aggregate function such as SUM in a query.

5. What does the term "impedance mismatch" refer to?

6. For the example database, write a query that determines the average price per category in the Dallas store, and the average price per category in the Chareston store and displays the complete list.

7. For the example database, find the name, price, and category of the highest priced item in each category.

8. Expand question number 6 to list each store's inventory of highest priced items. Is there one or more stores that are missing some high-priced items? Which stores and which items?

9. Can a table be joined to itself? If so, what technique must be used?

10. Explain how a correlated sub-query works.

11. What is the advantage of using an ORM tool and writing queries in an object query language? What are the disadvantages?

12. Why is "SELECT *" syntax inefficient?

ANSWER to the question in Figure 9-4:

```
SELECT Name AS 'Product Name', Price AS 'Item
Price', Description AS 'Item Description',
CategoryID AS 'Category Number'
FROM Product
```

APPENDIX C

■ ■ ■

Database Details

On the book's website there are SQL scripts available for download that will create and populate the example database in both MySQL and MS SQL Server Express. Due to slight syntax, naming, and design differences between the two there are two separate scripts for creating the database – one for each product. While scripts to seed the database with data are broken down into several scripts, they work both on both products. This section discusses the creation script differences and also shows examples of the INSERT statements, but the full content of the scripts is not given here. Also, this section is not meant to be a full tutorial on creating a database; it is merely an introduction to the topic with some brief samples.

Most databases follow a multi-part naming convention for their objects that is shown in full form as "Database.Schema.Object." Database is the name of the overall database, Schema is the name for a set of related objects within the database, and Object represents the name of the table or view. This full form is rarely used however; when a user logs into a database there is a default schema set for him/her and unless requesting data from another schema, both Database and Schema can be omitted from the query.

In the creation script for creating the database on MS SQL Server, the statements shown in Listing C-1 are used. This is ran by an administrator and will create the database named "StoreInventoryDB", a schema named "StoreInventory", a user/login named "store_user", and assign that user to have the default schema of "StoreInventory". When logging in as that user, the statement "SELECT * FROM Product" is the same as another user with a different default schema logging in and using "SELECT * FROM StoreInventory.Product" – both will bring back all records from the Product table.

Listing C-1. MS SQL Server Database Creation script

```
USE master
GO


-- Drop the database if it already exists
IF  EXISTS (SELECT name FROM sys.databases
            WHERE name = N'StoreInventoryDB')
    DROP DATABASE StoreInventoryDB
GO


CREATE DATABASE StoreInventoryDB
GO
```

```
-- USE THIS LOGIN/Password to access the database with the proper schema
defaults.
--
CREATE LOGIN store_user
        WITH PASSWORD = N'Pa$$wOrd';
GO

USE StoreInventoryDB
GO

CREATE SCHEMA StoreInventory
GO

CREATE USER store_user FOR LOGIN store_user
        WITH DEFAULT_SCHEMA = StoreInventory
GO

-- Add user to the database owner role
EXEC sp_addrolemember N'db_owner', N'store_user'
GO
```

Once the database has been created the table structure can be added. The script shown in Listing C-2 shows the creation of two tables, the second one being linked to the first via a FOREIGN KEY reference. This is a one-to-many reference and allows for the joining as described within Chapter 9.

Listing C-2. MS SQL Server object creation

```
IF OBJECT_ID('StoreInventory.Category', 'U') IS NOT NULL
  DROP TABLE StoreInventory.Category
GO
CREATE TABLE StoreInventory.Category
(
  idCategory INT IDENTITY(1,1) NOT NULL,
  Name VARCHAR(45) NOT NULL ,
  Description VARCHAR(90) NULL ,
  CONSTRAINT PK_CATEGORY PRIMARY KEY CLUSTERED (idCategory)
)
GO


-- ------------------------------------------------------
-- Table 'StoreInventory'.'Product'
-- ------------------------------------------------------
IF OBJECT_ID('StoreInventory.Product', 'U') IS NOT NULL
  DROP TABLE StoreInventory.Product
```

```
GO
CREATE  TABLE StoreInventory.Product (
  idProduct INT NOT NULL IDENTITY(1,1) ,
  Name VARCHAR(30) NOT NULL ,
  Price DECIMAL NOT NULL ,
  CategoryID INT NOT NULL ,
  Description VARCHAR(90) NULL ,
  CONSTRAINT PK_CATID PRIMARY KEY CLUSTERED (idProduct)
)
ALTER TABLE StoreInventory.Product
  WITH CHECK ADD CONSTRAINT CategoryID_Category
    FOREIGN KEY (CategoryID)
    REFERENCES StoreInventory.Category (idCategory)
GO
```

MySQL behaves a little differently in that "Database" and "Schema" are interchangeable and mean the same thing. This means that if a user has access to a particular database/schema the objects inside can simply be referenced by their name. Below is the creation script, both for the database and the same two tables shown before.

Listing C-3. MySQL Database and Table creation

```
CREATE SCHEMA IF NOT EXISTS StoreInventory DEFAULT CHARACTER SET latin1;
USE StoreInventory;


-- ------------------------------------------------------
-- Table 'StoreInventory'.'Category'
-- ------------------------------------------------------
CREATE  TABLE IF NOT EXISTS StoreInventory.Category (
  idCategory INT NOT NULL AUTO_INCREMENT ,
  Name VARCHAR(45) NOT NULL ,
  Description VARCHAR(90) NULL ,
  PRIMARY KEY (idCategory) )
ENGINE = InnoDB;


-- ------------------------------------------------------
-- Table 'StoreInventory'.'Product'
-- ------------------------------------------------------
CREATE  TABLE IF NOT EXISTS StoreInventory.Product (
  idProduct INT NOT NULL AUTO_INCREMENT ,
  Name VARCHAR(30) NOT NULL ,
  Price DECIMAL NOT NULL ,
  CategoryID INT NOT NULL ,
  Description VARCHAR(90) NULL ,
  PRIMARY KEY (idProduct) ,
  INDEX CategoryID (idProduct ASC) ,
```

```
  CONSTRAINT CategoryID_Category
    FOREIGN KEY (CategoryID )
    REFERENCES StoreInventory.Category (idCategory )
    ON DELETE NO ACTION
    ON UPDATE NO ACTION)
ENGINE = InnoDB;
```

Once the database and table structure are created, data is then seeded in with a series of INSERT statements. Notice the use of sub-queries to determine the proper foreign-key ID. Order is important; categories must be defined before products as products reference back to existing categories. The proper order for filling the data in the example database is Category, Product, Store, and finally Store_Product.

Listing C-4. Sample INSERT statements

```
INSERT INTO StoreInventory.Category (Name, Description)
VALUES ('Auto Parts', 'Parts and tools for automobiles');

INSERT INTO StoreInventory.Product (Name, Price, CategoryID, Description)
VALUES ( 'Battery', 100.00,
(select idCategory from StoreInventory.Category where name = 'Auto Parts'),
'Standard car battery' );

INSERT INTO StoreInventory.Product (Name, Price, CategoryID, Description)
VALUES ( 'Head Lamps', 25.00,
(select idCategory from StoreInventory.Category where name = 'Auto Parts'),
'Replacment head lamps' );

INSERT INTO StoreInventory.Product (Name, Price, CategoryID, Description)
VALUES ( 'Oil Filter', 6.00,
(select idCategory from StoreInventory.Category where name = 'Auto Parts'),
'Replacment oil filter' );
```

■ ■ ■

Bibliography

Books

Arking, J. and Millett, S. (2009). *Professional Enterprise .NET.* Indianapolis, IN: Wiley.

Fowler, M., et al. (1999). *Refactoring: Improving the Design of Existing Code.* Reading, MA: Addison-Wesley.

Gamma, E. et al. (1995). *Design Patterns: Elements of Reusable Object-Oriented Software.* Reading, MA: Addison-Wesley.

Kawalerowicz, M. and Berntson, C. (2011). *Continuous Integration in .NET.* Stamford, CT: Manning.

Kniberg, H. (2007). *Scrum and XP from the Trenches.* United States: C4 Media.

Loughran, E., and Hatcher, E. (2007). *Ant in Action: Java Development with Ant* (2nd Ed.) Stamford, CT: Manning.

Schwaber, K. (2004). *Agile Project Management with Scrum.* Redmond, WA: Microsoft Press.

Sonatype Company (2008). *Maven. The Definitive Guide.* Sebastopol, CA: O'Reilly Media.

Tahchiev, P., et al. (2010). *JUnit in Action* (2nd Ed.) Stamford, CT: Manning.

Wake, W. C. (2002). *Extreme Programming Explored.* Reading, MA: Addison-Wesley.

Walls, C. and Breidenbach, R. (2007) *Spring in Action* (2nd Ed.). Stamford, CT: Manning.

Wiegers, K. E. (2003). *Software Requirements* (2nd Ed.). Redmond, WA: Microsoft Press.

Wiegers, K. E. (2006). *More About Software Requirements.* Redmond, WA: Microsoft Press.

Web Sites

TIOBE Programming Community Index for August 2011. http://www.tiobe.com/index.php/content/paperinfo/tpci/index.html

Other Suggested Reading

Arlow, Jim (2005). *UML 2 and the Unified Process*. Reading, MA: Addison-Wesley

Hewardt, M. (2009). *Advanced .NET Debugging*. Reading, MA: Addison-Wesley.

Hunt, A. and Thomas, D. (1999). *The Pragmatic Programmer*. Reading, MA: Addison-Wesley.

Kerievsky, Joshua (2004). *Refactoring to Patterns*. Reading, MA: Addison-Wesley.

Mak, G., Long, J. and Rubio, D. (2010). *Spring Recipes* (2nd Ed). Berkley, CA: Apress.

Marshall, D. and Bruno, J. (2009). *Solid Code*. Redmond, WA: Microsoft Press.

Martin, R. (2008). *Clean Code: A Handbook of Agile Software Craftsmanship*. Boston, MA: Pearson.

McConnell, S. (2004). *Code Complete* (2nd Ed). Redmond, WA: Microsoft Press.

Osherove, R. (2009). *The Art of Unit Testing: with Examples in .NET*. Stamford, CT: Manning.

Pilone, D., Pitman, N. (2005) *UML 2.0 in a Nutshell*. Sebastopol, CA: O'Reilly Media, Inc.

Pugh, K. (2005). *Prefactoring*. Sebastopol, CA : O'Reilly Media, Inc.

Robbins, J. (2006). *Debugging Microsoft .NET 2.0 Applications* (3rd Ed). Redmond, WA: Microsoft Press.

Robert, M. C. and Micah, M. (2006). *Agile Principles, Patterns, and Practices in C#*. Boston, MA: Pearson.

Woodward, E., Surdek, S., and Ganis, M. (2010). *A Practical Guide to Distributed Scrum*. Boston, MA : Pearson.

SQL Additional Reading/Resources

Gennick, J. (2006). *SQL Pocket Guide*. Sebastopol, CA : O'Reilly Media, Inc.

Beaulieu, A. (2009). *Learning SQL*. Sebastopol, CA : O'Reilly Media, Inc.

Fehily, C. (2006). *SQL: Visual Quickstart Guide (3rd Ed)*. Berkeley, CA : Peachpit Press.

Jennings, R. (2009). *Professional ADO.NET 3.5 with LINQ and the Entity Framework*. Indianapolis, IN : Wiley Publishing, Inc.

Hamilton, B. (2008). *ADO.NET Cookbook, 2nd Edition*. Sebastopol, CA : O'Reilly Media, Inc.

Bales, D. (2003). *JDBC Pocket Reference*. Sebastopol, CA : O'Reilly Media, Inc.

Vibrant Publishers (2011). *JDBC Interview Questions You'll Most Likely be Asked*. Charleston, SC : Createspace Independent Publishing.

Elliot, J., O'Brien, T., and Fowler, R. (2008). *Harnessing Hibernate*. Sebastopol, CA : O'Reilly Media, Inc.

Index

Get the eBook for only $10!

Now you can take the weightless companion with you anywhere, anytime. Your purchase of this book entitles you to 3 electronic versions for only $10.

This Apress title will prove so indispensible that you'll want to carry it with you everywhere, which is why we are offering the eBook in 3 formats for only $10 if you have already purchased the print book.

Convenient and fully searchable, the PDF version enables you to easily find and copy code—or perform examples by quickly toggling between instructions and   applications. The MOBI format is ideal for your Kindle, while the ePUB can be utilized on a variety of mobile devices.

Go to www.apress.com/promo/tendollars to purchase your companion eBook.